CAMPUS TALK

Volume 1

Effective Communication Beyond the Classroom

Silvana Dushku
and
Paul Thompson

EDINBURGH
University Press

We owe a huge debt of gratitude to Karen Aijmer (University of Gothenburg, Sweden), Ronald Carter (University of Nottingham, UK), and Wayne B. Dickerson and Erica McClure (both University of Illinois at Urbana–Champaign) for inspiring and encouraging us to write this book.

Edinburgh University Press is one of the leading university presses in the UK. We publish academic books and journals in our selected subject areas across the humanities and social sciences, combining cutting-edge scholarship with high editorial and production values to produce academic works of lasting importance. For more information visit our website: edinburghuniversitypress.com

Edinburgh University Press Ltd
The Tun – Holyrood Road, 12(2f) Jackson's Entry, Edinburgh EH8 8PJ

Typeset in Baskerville
by Biblichor Ltd, Edinburgh,
and printed and bound in Great Britain.

A CIP record for this book is available from the British Library

ISBN 978 1 4744 1936 9 (hardback)
ISBN 978 1 4744 1937 6 (webready PDF)
ISBN 978 1 4744 1938 3 (paperback)
ISBN 978 1 4744 1939 0 (epub)

CONTENTS

INTRODUCTION

Campus Talk is a research-based guide for upper-intermediate/advanced adult learners of English (Common European Framework of Reference (CEFR) B1–C2) to promote interactional language awareness and develop active listening skills and strategies. It aims at enhancing learners' appropriate English language use, and facilitating their everyday social communication in both academic and non-academic environments on campus.

The two-volume *Campus Talk* textbook can be used as a self-reference guide and practice resource by individual learners or as an English as a Second/Foreign Language (ESL/EFL) textbook in the classroom. It is designed to meet the English language development needs of a wide range of learners, including but not limited to:

- international students who intend to complete undergraduate and/or graduate studies in an English-speaking country
- international teaching assistants (ITAs)
- exchange and post-doctoral students, as well as visiting scholars who study, work, and/or conduct research in an English-speaking country
- learners who need to take the Test of English for International Communication (TOEIC) or C1 Advanced (CAE) tests.

Through a learner need-based syllabus, *Campus Talk*:

- ensures that the learners are exposed to the most salient and widely used lexico-grammatical patterns of spoken English discourse, in and outside academia, that are pertinent to their level
- provides plenty of opportunities to practice and assess interactive listening skills and strategies
- facilitates conversation management by providing knowledge of and practice in conversation maintenance strategies in a variety of situations
- promotes practice of common speech act routines with a focus on interaction rather than on speaker turns

- encourages learners' observation skills and noticing through language corpus investigation and analysis of everyday situational language use
- enhances awareness of a wide range of communication strategies that learners can use to interact fluently, confidently, and effectively
- draws learners' attention to socio-cultural aspects of communication in English and how they affect interaction
- promotes learners' self-reflection and independent management of their learning through learner error analysis and self-assessment tools.

Campus Talk is comprised of two volumes. Each volume contains four instructional units and each unit consists of three topic-/skill-related parts or mini-units. The unit introduction highlights the unit goals and concrete learner benefits. Each unit includes interactional tasks and activities which provide plenty of opportunities for observation and practice. There is a set of self-study exercises in each unit, too. The unit tasks and activities culminate in the **unit main speaking task**. Each unit has a **self-assessment** section at the end, which invites the learners to track and reflect upon their unit benefits and progress made. The usage-informed **vocabulary list**, also located at the end of each unit, is intended for use by the learner for self-study and classroom practice. The unit is completed with a **unit quiz** to test learner's understanding.

The learning goals for each unit of *Campus Talk* Volume 1 are as follows:

Unit 1

In this unit, students learn to:

- strike up and engage in a conversation with attention to audience and the situation
- share and respond to good/bad news appropriately
- manage small talk in formal/informal situations.

Unit 2

In this unit, students learn to:

- manage group communication with attention to turns, participant roles, and time
- express and react to an opinion (including nuanced agreement/disagreement)
- make and respond to a suggestion/recommendation.

Unit 3

In this unit, students learn to:

- express and respond to positive feelings (such as joy and enthusiasm) with appropriate delivery
- express and respond to negative feelings (such as anger) with appropriate delivery
- talk about feelings; express degrees of feelings through common idiomatic/semi-idiomatic expressions).

Unit 4

In this unit, students learn to:

- make and respond to pre-requests and direct requests face to face or on the phone
- make, understand, and respond to indirect requests
- use hedgers to soften requests.

Each unit contains a number of listening activities. The MP3 files for the listening activities can be accessed on the **student's companion website**, which complements this book. In the book, an icon appears in the text to show where there is a listening file available.

Several units contain a language corpus investigation activity. The corpora used are the Corpus of Contemporary American English (COCA; available at <https://www.english-corpora.org/coca/> (last accessed October 22, 2020)), and the Michigan Corpus of Academic Spoken English (MICASE; available at <https://quod.lib.umich.edu/cgi/c/corpus/corpus>, (last accessed October 22, 2020)), and for each activity there is also an online screencast to help demonstrate the procedures for doing the activity. An icon appears in the text for the activity to indicate that there is a screencast. These screencasts can be found on the **student's companion website**.

The *Campus Talk* student's companion website (https://campustalk.online/) also offers an **online workbook** for students, with supplementary activities and language practice resources.

In addition, a *Teacher's Notes* booklet is downloadable via the **Edinburgh University Press website** (edinburghuniversitypress.com/campustalk1). This booklet contains guidance on the purpose of each activity in *Campus Talk* and suggests ways to structure the activity in class.

EXPLANATION OF ICONS USED IN THE BOOKS

MP3 file for listening activity is available on the Edinburgh University Press website (edinburghuniversitypress.com/campustalk1).

Screencast for corpus investigation activity is available on the Edinburgh University Press website (edinburghuniversitypress.com/campustalk1).

ACKNOWLEDGMENTS

Photo acknowledgments

Priscilla Du Preez on Unsplash (page 3)
Hivan Arvizu @soyhivan on Unsplash (page 4)
Victor Freitas on Unsplash (page 7)
Charles Postiaux on Unsplash (page 9)
Linda Dushku (page 12)
Brianna Corletto (page 15)
Helena Lopes on Unsplash (page 18)
Ani Dushku (page 21)
Product School on Unsplash (page 24)
Helena Lopes on Unsplash (page 41)
Brooke Cagle on Unsplash (page 43)
Priscilla Du Preez on Unsplash (page 44)
Dylan Gillis on Unsplash (page 47)
Anna Vander Stel on Unsplash (page 51)
Marvin Meyer on Unsplash (page 53)
Headway on Unsplash (page 54)
Shane Rounce on Unsplash (page 56)
Charles Deluvio on Unsplash (page 62)
National Sculptors' Guild on Unsplash (page 79)
Priscilla Du Preez on Unsplash (page 80)
Jordan Whitt on Unsplash (page 84)
Jon Tyson on Unsplash (page 86)
Raychan on Unsplash (page 90)
Mimi Thian on Unsplash (page 92)
Steve Johnson on Unsplash (page 93)
Jennifer Brown-Rocheleau (page 96)
Iga Palacz on Unsplash (page 98)
Jennifer Brown-Rocheleau (page 103)

Jennifer Brown-Rocheleau (page 119)
Mimi Thian on Unsplash (page 122)
Jennifer Brown-Rocheleau (page 125)
Fezbot2000 on Unsplash (page 128)
Jennifer Brown-Rocheleau (page 131)
Food Photographer Jennifer Pallian on Unsplash (page 134)
Ervin Mazniku (page 135)
Kristina Flour on Unsplash (page 138)

Recording acknowledgments

Musical intro to audio files is extracted from Modern Jazz Samba by Kevin Macleod (incompetency.com). Licensed under Creative Commons: By Attribution 3.0 License http://creativecommons.org/licenses/by/3.0/
Sound engineer (Urbana–Champaign): Liam Moran
Sound engineer (Birmingham): Gabriela Zogall
Vocal talents (Urbana–Champaign): Evan Branson, Jennifer Brown-Rocheleau, Peter Chiligiris, Anita Greenfield, Hillary Veitch
Vocal talents (Birmingham): Natalia Barton, Luis Freija Escudero, Grace Harding, Brittany Moster, Peter De Sanctis, Sara Cardoso Saraiva, Niamh Scattergood.

General acknowledgments for help with trialing, critiquing, or reviewing in the development of the book

Kristin Bouton, Jennifer Brown-Rocheleau, Joy Chen-Howard, Peter Chiligiris, Brianna Corletto, Maggie Courtright, Kate Curry, Anisa Dalle, Ani Dushku, Susan Feldman, Julieta Fernandez, Pam Fernandez, Patricia Ferrer, Megan Ficek, Gretchen Forman, Sue Ingels, Kallie-Jo Ho, Andy Hunt, Anna Kasten, Dustin Kelly, Jill Knutson, Irena Kola, Lynee Lawson, Mary-Jo Licht, Erica McClure, Natalie Mullen, Rachel Newell, Ulugbek Nurmukhamedov, Lisa Ochoa, Carleen Sacris, LuAnn Sorenson, Jeanette Pyne, Patricia Watts, Aziz Yuldashev, Ellen Zlotnik.

UNIT 1: CONNECTING WITH EACH OTHER

IN THIS UNIT, YOU WILL LEARN TO:

- **PART 1:** Strike up a conversation
- **PART 2:** Share and respond to news
- **PART 3:** Make small talk/chat

Final Unit Task: With a partner, record an unrehearsed small talk/chat online or face to face.

PART 1:
Striking up a conversation

Activity 1: Let's Get Started

A DISCUSS – You are going to listen to a conversation among people at a party. Before you listen, discuss the following questions with your partner:

1. **In your country, how do you start a conversation with**
   a. people you don't know?
   b. friends?

2. **If you have been in an English-speaking country, have you had any difficulties in striking up conversation with**
   a. native speakers?
   b. others?

B LISTEN AND IDENTIFY – Susan is having a party at her place with some of her new school friends. Listen to their conversations. In pairs, identify and complete the table below with examples of conversation-opening words and phrases:

Listening file: Unit_1_Part_1_Activity_1B.mp3

Conversation openings	Examples
Greetings (e.g., "Hi! How are you")	
Forms of address (e.g., names)	
Questions (e.g., "Have we met before?")	
Comments (e.g., a compliment: "Nice shoes!")	
News pre-announcements (e.g., "Guess what?")	

C SHARE AND DISCUSS – Get together with another pair. Share your examples of the conversation-opening expressions with them and complete the information in the table above. Discuss their usage according to the situation and speakers.

Activity 2: Let's Review: Greetings, Responses, and Follow-up

A REVIEW – Based on your own language experience, complete and match the following opening turns in a conversation. Conversation 1 has been completed for you.

	Speaker's greeting	Listener's response	Listener's follow-up
1.	*What's up?*	*Nothing.*	*What's up with you?*
2.			Yourself?
3.		Not a whole lot.	
4.	What's going on?		
5.		Not too bad.	
6.	Hey, what are you up to?		
7.			New hairstyle?
8.		Doing good.	
9.			I haven't seen you in a million years!
10.			Nice earrings!

B PRACTICE – Take turns to practice greetings, responses, and follow-up in a ball game. Toss the ball to each other. As you toss it, use a greeting. When you catch it, give an appropriate response followed by a comment or question to keep the conversation going.

Activity 3: Forms of Address – Focus on Usage

A ANALYZE AND DISCUSS – Log in to the Corpus of Contemporary American English (COCA). Choose the spoken section. Search for two of the forms of address in the table below, as assigned by the teacher. With your partner, analyze the first twenty examples of these forms of address in context. Discuss their uses and enter the required information in the table below.

Form of address	Speaker's gender (circle one)	Gender of the addressee (circle one)	Speaker's relationship with the addressee (circle one)
(You) guys	Male Female	Male Female	Formal Informal
Dude	Male Female	Male Female	Formal Informal
Hey man	Male Female	Male Female	Formal Informal
Buddy	Male Female	Male Female	Formal Informal
Sir	Male Female	Male Female	Formal Informal
Ma'am	Male Female	Male Female	Formal Informal
Sweetheart	Male Female	Male Female	Formal Informal

B SHARE AND DISCUSS – Share the results of your analysis with another pair. Switch pairs until you complete the table with the information on all the other forms of address. Discuss the findings in class. How are these forms of address similar or different in usage? Provide examples from the COCA corpus.

CORPUS BOX

Forms of address like "dude" and "buddy" are called "familiarizers." They show some degree of closeness between the speaker and audience. They can also be used among strangers. The opposite of a familiarizer is an honorific, such as "Sir."

British linguist Geoffrey Leech compared frequency of use of such forms of address in American and British English, and he used corpus evidence to do this. A corpus is a large collection of samples of natural language use, and linguists use these to find out about distributions of linguistic features. Leech found that these forms of address are 25 percent more frequent in American English, and also that Americans use familiarizers much more often than the British do.

"Buddy" – "Hey man" – "Dude": Which of these forms of address is more common in spoken American English? In the Santa Barbara Corpus of Spoken American English, the most common familiarizer is "dude," followed by "hey man."

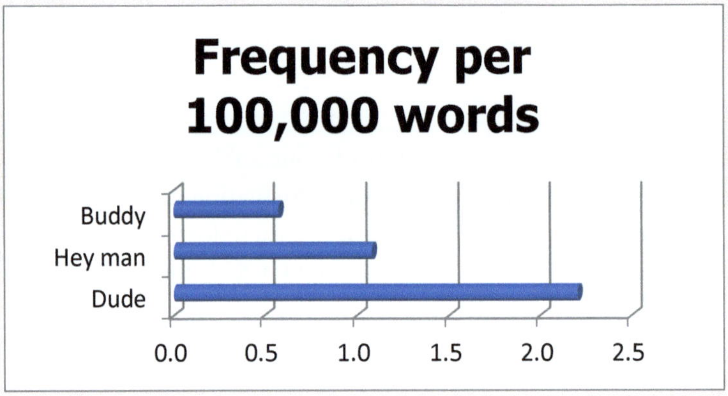

Listen carefully to the spoken English being used around you, on television, or in movies. Which forms of address do you hear most often?

Activity 4: Forms of Address – What Else Can They Tell You?

A LISTEN AND INFER – Listen to each dialogue between various speakers in different situations. Analyze the language they use and check (✓) the appropriate box to describe each speaker's relationship to the listener.

Listening file: Unit_1_Part_1_Activity_4A.mp3

	Dialogue	Relationship with listener	Speaker's emotional state
1.	A: [Finds a big mess in his dorm room] **Guys**! What's going on here? B Nothing, just trying to get rid of stuff!	☐ Formal ☐ Informal	
2.	A **You guys**! You really shouldn't have. Thank you so much! B No problem! Enjoy!	☐ Formal ☐ Informal	
3.	A I'm going to be honest with you, **buddy**. You really shouldn't have said anything. B Oh, come on! No big deal!	☐ Formal ☐ Informal	
4.	A **Hey buddy**, are you lost? B [Crying] I can't find my Mommy!	☐ Formal ☐ Informal	
5.	A **Dude**, how much time do we have left? B Two minutes only! Hurry!	☐ Formal ☐ Informal	
6.	A **Dude!** Just chill, OK? B I really can't stand it when people cut in line like this!	☐ Formal ☐ Informal	
7.	A **Hey man**, watch out. Those things can walk, you know. [The other person forgot his iPhone on the counter] B Oops! Thanks!	☐ Formal ☐ Informal	
8.	A You can't do this to me, **man**! Why didn't you tell me? B Just didn't wanna (want to) bother you.	☐ Formal ☐ Informal	
9.	A Excuse me, is this the way to the Lincoln Museum? B [Policeman] Yes, **Ma'am**. Just keep right.	☐ Formal ☐ Informal	
10.	A Mom, I'm late! Is the sandwich ready? B Yes, **Ma'am**! Here you go!	☐ Formal ☐ Informal	

B LISTEN AND INFER – Listen again. Focus on the form of address in each dialogue. What does it tell you about the speaker's emotional state? Use an adjective to describe the emotion (for example, angry, disappointed, empathetic, and so on). Share with your partner.

Listening file: Unit_1_Part_1_Activity_4B.mp3

PART 2: Sharing and responding to news

Activity 1: Talking About What's New

A LISTEN AND RESPOND – Linda and Janet are drinking sodas and chatting at a campus café. Listen to the conversation and answer the following questions:

Listening file: Unit_1_Part_2_Activity_1A.mp3

1. What is the relationship between the speakers?
2. What does Janet say to break the news to Linda?

B **LISTEN AND ANALYZE –** Listen to the conversation again. What news about Christmas do Linda and Janet share? How do they respond to the news? Complete the table below.

Listening file: Unit_1_Part_2_Activity_1B.mp3

News		Response	
Linda's plans		Janet's response to Linda's news	
Janet's plans		Linda's response to Janet's news	

C BRAINSTORM – Can you think of other words/phrases to announce or respond to the news emotionally? What role does their intonation play to convey surprise or evaluation? Work with your partner and complete the table below.

	Pre-announcements	**Response**	
		Surprise	*Evaluation*
Good news	You won't believe what happened . . .	Really? Wow!	Great!
Bad news	I don't know how to tell you this, but . . .	Oh, no!	That's too bad!

Activity 2: News Breaking and Responses – Let's Practice

ROLE-PLAY – List a couple of events/facts (good/bad news) you might like to share. (They do not need to be true. Improvise!) With your partner, role-play announcing and responding to them. Exchange roles. Make sure that you listen and respond actively.

Good news: ______________________________

Good news: ______________________________

Bad news: ______________________________

Bad news: ______________________________

ELLIPSIS IN CASUAL CONVERSATION

In casual conversation, we often leave out words and reduce sentence structure because we believe that the listener knows what we are talking about, and/or the situation makes it clear. This language reduction is called "ellipsis." For example:

A: How are you?
B: Pretty good! (I am pretty good). You? (How about you?/How are you?)

Elliptical language is so common that it makes the use of complete utterances in response to some questions sound really formal and unnatural. For example, compare person B statements in each conversation:

A: Do you know I am moving to Paris for good?
B: No, I did not know that you are moving to Paris for good. When are you leaving?

A: Do you know I am moving to Paris for good?
B: No! When?

Activity 3: Ellipsis – Let's Make It Real

A LISTEN AND DISCUSS – Listen to this news-sharing conversation between friends. Does it sound natural? Why? Discuss with your partner.

Listening file: Unit_1_Part_2_Activity_3A.mp3

B READ AND ANALYZE – Now look at the conversation script below (the left column only) to check your impressions. What do you notice?

A: Do you know I have good news to share with you?

B: No, I don't know. What is the good news?

A: The college gave me a research assistantship for the spring semester!

B: This is really good news! I congratulate you on it.

A: Thank you. I am also happy because I do not have to teach again next semester.

B: Oh, yes, I understand how you feel about teaching. It is always an exhausting effort. That is great!

A: Thank you. I have to go now. My class will start in a few minutes. I hope to see you later.

B: Yes, I understand it. I will see you around.

Original conversation	**Rewritten conversation**
A: Do you know I have good news to share with you?	
B: No, I don't know. What is the good news?	
A: The college gave me a research assistantship for the spring semester!	
B: This is really good news! I congratulate you on it.	
A: Thank you. I am also happy because I do not have to teach again next semester.	
B: Oh, yes, I understand how you feel about teaching. It is always an exhausting effort. That is great!	
A: Thank you. I have to go now. My class will start in a few minutes. I hope to see you later.	
B: Yes, I understand it. I will see you around.	

C REWRITE AND ROLE-PLAY – With your partner, rewrite each turn in the conversation below paying attention to sentence structure and length. Role-play the improved conversation.

PART 3:
Making small talk/chatting

Activity 1: Let's Review: Small Talk Topics

A LISTEN AND INFER – Ani is waiting for some friends at a coffee shop when she runs into Mathew, her classmate. They make small talk. Listen to their conversation and write down their small talk topics. What do you think motivates their choice of topics? Check (√) the right box or boxes below.

Listening file: Unit_1_Part_3_Activity_1A.mp3

Small talk topics	Interest in listener	Shared knowledge of one another	Shared knowledge of the immediate surroundings	Shared interests	Politeness	Comfort with topic/ participant	Other?
Weather			√			√	

B LISTEN AND DISCUSS – Listen again and discuss the following questions in groups.

Listening file: Unit_1_Part_3_Activity_1A.mp3

1. Are the topics appropriate to the situation and participants? Explain why.
2. What other topics could be appropriate in this small talk? Name a few.
3. Do you consider Ani's question about Emma appropriate or inappropriate? Explain why.
4. Can you think of topics that would be inappropriate to bring up in such a conversation? Give examples.
5. How similar or different would topics in small talk between students be in your culture? Explain.

C CHOOSE AND ROLE-PLAY – Your academic adviser has invited you over for dinner. List one small talk topic that you can use, and one that you should avoid with the following people you meet at his place. (The first one is done for you.) With your partner, use two appropriate topics from the list and role-play small talk situations.

People at the dinner party	Appropriate topic	Inappropriate topic
Your adviser's middle-aged wife	Food	Age
Your adviser's graduate research assistant		
A new female professor in your department		
Your adviser's teenager son		
Your former statistics professor		
Your department's secretary who retired recently		
Your department head		

Activity 2: Keeping the Conversation Going – Focus on Strategies

A LISTEN AND IDENTIFY – Ani and her friends are hanging out at the Student Union after school. Listen to their conversation. Which of the following strategies do they use to keep the conversation going? Identify who uses the strategy (Ani, Jessica, Paul) in the first column in the table on the next page. Include an example of what they do or say in the third column:

Listening file: Unit_1_Part_3_Activity_2A.mp3

Speakers	Conversation maintenance strategies	Examples
	Questions (e.g., clarification questions)	
	Comments (e.g., surprise or evaluation words/ phrases such as "*Wow!*" or "*That's great!*")	
	Continuers (e.g., "*Uh-uh,*" "*OK,*" "*Right*")	
	Summary of the speaker's statement/ message (e.g., to show your understanding and, possibly, make a comment on it)	
	Topic change (e.g., to avoid an awkward or embarrassing situation)	
	Repetitions of the speaker's words (e.g., "*New York?* Wow, that's awesome!"	

B MATCH AND EXPAND – Complete the conversations by matching the speaker's statement with the appropriate listener's conversation strategy in the box. Then, think of a possible speaker's response/reaction to it. Write it down in the third column below. The first one is done for you.

You mean, you've been living here for over two decades? Wow!

Did he? That's weird.

Uh-huh. So, you had to, I guess.

That's great. Do you plan to continue your graduate studies or get a job soon?

Really? So, it must get pretty hot here.

That's alright, I got it. So, how is school and everything?

No worries. Please stay as long as you can, OK?

Speaker's statement	Listener's conversation maintenance strategies	Speaker's new turn
Sorry I couldn't return this the other day.	*That's alright, I got it. So, how is school and everything?*	*School's fine. Just getting ready for the Spring Break.*
This is still a fairly normal summer we're having.		
Sorry, but I am not going to be able to attend the entire graduation ceremony.		
I got a job at this university right after graduation in 1995.		
I studied computer science in my country for 5 years.		
He acted like he'd never seen us before.		
And he's like, "I would rewrite it."		

C RESPOND AND ROLE-PLAY – This is your first meeting with other graduate teaching assistants in your department. After introducing yourself, you get to chat with some of them. How do you keep the conversation going? Complete the right column in the table on the page opposite.
Role-play three of the situations with your partner. Switch roles.

Name	S/he says . . .	You say . . .
Sarah	This is my second year in the program.	
Ben	Well, the first couple of weeks are a bit overwhelming . . .	
Sue	I bet you're going to enjoy teaching!	
Jim	You've got to join our biking club on Saturdays.	
Rachel	I've taught English 101 for three semesters now.	
Jill	I'm going to enroll you to my course site and you can check all you need.	

Activity 3: Let's Review: Ending the Conversation

A COMPLETE – Now look again at the conversation among Ani, Jessica, and Paul in Activity 2. How does it end? Use the conversation script provided below to finish their conversation. Choose appropriate pre-closings (phrases used before ending the conversation) and closings ("goodbye" expressions) from the table.

Pre-closing	Closing
Gotta go. (Got to go)	Bye.
Got to run.	See you/ya.
I'd better get going.	Take care.
I'd better let you go.	(See/Catch you) Later.
Sorry, I have to leave. Let's do coffee sometime.	I left it.
So good to see you!	Take it easy.

Ani: Excuse me. [looks at her cell phone] That's Rob telling me he's waiting for me outside. Sorry, guys. Gotta go now.
Paul: ______________________________.
Jessica: ______________________________.
Ani: ______________________________. [goes]
Jessica: [looks at her cell phone] Wow, it's 8 already.
Paul: Oh, yeah?
Jessica: Yeah, and I still have to stop at the grocery store. ______________.
Paul: ______________________________.
Jessica: ______________________________.

B LISTEN AND DISCUSS – Now listen to the ending of their conversation. Is it very different from your completed conversation ending above? Discuss in pairs.

Listening file: Unit_1_Part_3_Activity_3B.mp3

C ANALYZE AND CORRECT – Check the following conversation endings with your partner. Is there anything wrong with them? If "yes," correct it.

1.	A: Take care. B: Why? Is there something wrong with me?	5.	A: Have a good afternoon. B: Yeah, you, too. Have a nice day! See you tomorrow! Bye!
2.	A: It was good to talk to you. B: Yeah, me, too!	6.	A: Have a good day. B: You do the same now.
3.	A: Nice meeting you. B: Yeah, likewise.	7.	A: Have a good trip. B: Yeah, have a good trip.
4.	A: Enjoy the Break! B: I'm going to try.	8.	A: I'll catch ya around! B: OK.

Take a moment to reflect. Do you recognize any of your own errors with closings now?

UNIT 1
Final Unit Task

A **ROLE-PLAY –** With a partner, record an unrehearsed small talk/chat online or face to face.

While recording, make sure you:

a. start the conversation naturally (use conversation-opening words/phrases)

b. choose relevant conversation topics (bring up topics related to your shared interests, knowledge, comfort in conversation, and so on)

c. use appropriate conversation topics (avoid "taboo" topics such as marital status, salary, religion)

d. keep the conversation going actively (use body language, show surprise or evaluation, ask questions, and so on)

e. end the conversation smoothly (use pre-closing and closing words/phrases).

B EVALUATE – Watch/listen to your recorded small talk/chat. Use the following guidelines to evaluate your performance. How did you do?

Performance evaluation criteria	Yes	To some extent	No
1. Did you start the conversation naturally?			
2. Were the conversation topics relevant?	√		
3. Were the conversation topics appropriate?			
4. Did you actively keep the conversation going?			
5. Did you end the conversation smoothly?			
6. Did you speak clearly?			
7. Overall, was your conversation natural?			

I would like to improve:

1. ______________________________

2. ______________________________

UNIT 1 SELF-ASSESSMENT: What Progress Did I Make?

1 Review Unit 1 vocabulary list and complete the table below.

	Expressions I can actively use	Expressions I need to review
Part 1: Strike up a conversation		
Part 2: Share and respond to news		
Part 3: Make small talk/chat		

II These are the conversation strategies you practiced in this unit. Check (✓) the box in the category that best evaluates your ability to use them.

Strategy	Very well	Fairly well	Not very well
I can greet and respond to a greeting	☐	☐	☐
I can use a conversation starter other than a greeting (e.g., a question, a compliment, and so on)	☐	☐	☐
I can choose appropriate conversation topics	☐	☐	☐
I can use a news pre-announcer (e.g., “Guess what?”)	☐	☐	☐
I can share news	☐	☐	☐
I can respond to the news	☐	☐	☐
I can keep the conversation going	☐	☐	☐
I can pre-close the conversation	☐	☐	☐
I can end the conversation	☐	☐	☐

III Write about what you learned in this unit, and what you plan to continue to work on:

One new skill/strategy I learned in this unit is:

What I plan to continue to work on is:

UNIT 1
VOCABULARY LIST

Use the chart below to study the new unit vocabulary and record any new topic-related vocabulary from this unit and elsewhere.

Topic/Function	Vocabulary to review	New vocabulary
Greetings and responses	What's up? Not much. How're you doing? Doing well. How's it going? Great! How've you been? OK. Busy!	What've you been up to? What's going on? Nothing. How're things? Great! Hi/Hey there! Hi!/Hey!
Forms of address	Hey guys Miss/Ms Ma'am Sir	Dude Buddy Bro Girl
Pre-announcers	Guess what? Did you hear about . . . ? Do you know what happened? Did I tell you that . . . ? Have you heard . . . ?	You won't believe this! Here's the thing. You know what? I didn't tell you, did I, that . . .
Expressions of surprise	Oh my God! Oh, no! Oh, man! Really? Wow! Are you serious?	Are you kidding (me)? You're kidding me! You've got to be kidding me! For real? No way! Get out (of here)!

(Table continued eoverleaf)

Topic/Function	Vocabulary to review	New vocabulary
Expressions of evaluation	(That's) crazy/too bad/terrible/awful. How embarrassing! (That's) right/true/good/correct/great/fine/OK/important/cool/crazy/awesome/amazing/wonderful/fantastic.	That's a pain/a nightmare/a shame. What a pain/a shame/a mess/a hassle. Good for you!
Conversation pre-closing expressions	It was so nice (great/wonderful) to see you. Well, it was really nice talking to you. Wow, it's getting late. Let's get together again soon. I'm sorry, but I really have to go now. It was good to see you. Nice/Great talking to you.	Well, I'd better be going. I have a lot of homework to do tonight. I'd better let you go. Gotta (got to) go. Likewise.
Conversation closing expressions	Have a good weekend. Good luck on your test/with your new project. Have a nice trip. Safe travels. See you. See ya. Bye. Good night.	Take care! (I'll) see you around. Have a good one. Catch you later.

UNIT 1
QUIZ

Activity 1

Listen and complete the conversation turns below. What could person B say? Person B's response should match person A's turns.

Listening file: Unit_1_Quiz_1.mp3

1.	**A** We are going to Europe for the summer. How cool is that! **B:** A: Italy and Spain.	**3.**	**A:** Oh my God! **B:** A: Take a look. It must have snowed all night.
2.	**A:** Hey, what've you been up to? **B:** **A:** Same. Just studying.	**4.**	**A:** Sorry for all this trouble. **B:** **A:** Thanks! I'm glad I talked to you.

Activity 2

Listen to the statement and circle the most appropriate response that best leads to further conversation:

Listening file: Unit_1_Quiz_2.mp3

1.	(Two friends at the bus stop) **A:** I have been wanting to watch this new movie "Indigo." **B:** a. Oh, really? What's it like? b. Oh, really? When will that be? c. Oh, really? What's it about?	**3.**	(Two colleagues in the break room) **A:** The weather has been so horrible lately. **B:** a. Not really. b. No kidding! I wonder how long it will last. c. Why do you think so?
2.	(Two new faculty at a dinner party at a colleague's place) **A:** Hello. I don't believe we've met. **B:** a. Yes, we have. b. No, we haven't. Do I know you? c. No, I don't think so. You must be Ani's sister, right?	**4.**	(Two students at a holiday party) **A:** This is a fun party! **B:** a. Yes it is. Did you get to try the food? b. Really? Why do you like it? c. Actually, it is a little boring.

Activity 3

Listen to the elliptical phrases people frequently use to respond to greetings. Write down a greeting that matches each elliptical response you hear. Do not use the same greeting more than once.

Listening file: Unit_1_Quiz_3.mp3

Greeting	Elliptical response
1.	1. Not much.
2.	2. OK, I guess.
3.	3. Nothing.
4.	4. Not too bad.
5.	5. Pretty good.

Activity 4

Match the responses on the left with the conversation pre-closings on the right. Place the response number next to the appropriate statement. There is one extra response.

	Response	Statement	
1.	Sounds good.	So good to see you!	
2.	Never mind.	I need to go, but let's do lunch sometime.	
3.	OK. I'll catch you later.	So, I'll see you at 5 in the library then?	
4.	Good to see you, too.	I'll have to get going.	
5.	Sure thing! I'll be there.		

UNIT 2:
PUTTING YOUR HEADS TOGETHER

IN THIS UNIT, YOU WILL LEARN TO:

- **PART 1:** Manage group communication
- **PART 2:** Express and react to an opinion
- **PART 3:** Make and respond to a suggestion/ recommendation

Final Unit Task: Role-play a group discussion of a student proposal for a school/community development project.

PART 1:
Managing group communication

Activity 1: Let's Get Started

A **DESCRIBE** – Think of how you commonly talk in activities such as class discussions, group work, and study groups in your country. Complete the table on the next page with your answers to the questions on each aspect of student group communication. Share them with a partner.

Features	Student group communication
Turn taking Who talks first? Who talks next? How is this done?	
Voice volume High or low? When does the voice volume change?	
Eye contact Do you maintain eye contact?	
Body language Do you use facial expressions, body movements, hand gestures? How?	
Level of formality Are these conversations formal or informal?	
Politeness Are polite phrases (Example: *Please*; *Sorry*; *Thank you*) used in these conversations?	

B LISTEN AND COMPARE – Students discuss their group survey presentation assignment on friendship and dating. Listen and take notes. How different or similar is it to student group communication in your country? Make a list of differences and/or similarities. Share with a partner.

Listening file: Unit_2_Part_1_Activity_1B.mp3

Differences	Similarities
1.	1.
2.	2.

Activity 2: Group Communication Skills

A IDENTIFY – With a partner, fill out the chart opposite with one or two expressions that can be used in the group work situations described below. See the given examples.

	Group work situation	**What can you say?**
1.	Students are eager to participate and they talk all at the same time.	Hey, can we go one at a time? Ben, you were saying . . .
2.	One student dominates the talk and does not give others a chance to participate.	

	Group work situation	What can you say?
3.	Your group is running out of time.	Hey guys, how much time do we have now?
4.	One student in your group is off-task.	
5.	One student is very shy. She/he is afraid of making mistakes, so she/he remains silent.	
6.	One student seems to prefer to give only brief explanations or yes/no answers.	
7.	One student talks to other students in his/her native language all the time.	
8.	One student insists she/he has all the correct answers.	

B **SHARE AND IMPROVE –** Share your completed chart with another pair of students. Improve your chart by adding other expressions you may learn from them.

Activity 3: Having a Group Discussion

The School Alumni Foundation is donating ten thousand dollars for a school/community development project. The School Board has invited each class to submit a student project proposal.

A **DISCUSS –** In groups of three, discuss several development project options. What could benefit your school or your community the most? Brainstorm. Take notes of opinions about possible projects. Video-record the discussion.

Project	Description	Opinions
Option 1		
Option 2		

B **WATCH AND ANALYZE –** Watch the recorded discussion and analyze your group members' roles in it. When communicating with one another, did you or your group members use any of the expressions reviewed in Activity 2 above? If "yes," give an example. Make a suggestion about how to further improve group communication.

I heard: ______________________________

We could ______________________________

Activity 4: Managing Turns in Conversation

A LISTEN AND ANALYZE – Students are working on a class assignment in a group. Listen to their conversations and take notes. Then, answer the following questions about their group communication.

Listening file: Unit_2_Part_1_Activity_4A.mp3

1. What do the students talk about?
2. Do they all share the same opinion on each choice?
3. Is there a group leader who manages the group discussion (for example, he/she may distribute turns, keep track of time, etc.)?
4. How would you describe the students' turn-taking "behavior"? What does it say about their engagement in this task?
5. Identify examples of turn interruptions and interjections. Describe how they are used in conversation.

B SHARE – Get together in a group of three students. Share your answers with your group members.

DID YOU KNOW THAT . . . ?

Listening file: Unit_2_Part_1_Activity_4_box.mp3

You can take a turn in English when you observe the speaker's:

- voice pitch going down
  Example: That's just a thought.
- voice volume decreasing
  Example: Of course I could do it.
- last syllable in an utterance getting longer
  Example: I was mAd!
- utterance ending with "er," "you know"
  Example: It was tough, you know.
- gestures/facial expressions showing end of his/her turn
  Example: Oh, well . . . (facial expression and shoulder shrugging)
- pause at the end of an utterance
  Example: That's it.

When we talk, we often make hesitation pauses, and try to use "pause fillers" such as "well" and "er."
Example: Well, I'm not sure where to begin.

Can you think of other pause fillers? Write them in the space below:

Also, we sometimes stop to organize our thoughts and make planning pauses.
Example: Well, that's a good question. (Pause) Let me think for a minute . . .
In English conversation, hesitation or planning pauses are NOT opportunities for the listener.

C **REFLECT –** What about in your culture? When can you take a turn when communicating in a group? Take notes. Share your thoughts with your group.

PART 2:
Expressing and reacting to an opinion

Activity 1: Expressing Certainty/Uncertainty

DID YOU KNOW THAT . . . ?

Listening file: Unit_2_Part_1_Activity_1_box.mp3

The phrases we use the most to express various degrees of certainty when exchanging opinions are:

- **I think** — **Example: It's kind of cold, I think.**
- **I don't know** — **Example: I don't know, but this seems a bit strange to me.**
- **I know** — **Example: I know, working and studying is not easy.**
- **I guess** — **Example: The battery is dead, I guess.**
- **I bet** — **Example: I bet you'll love it!**

A LISTEN AND GUESS – Listen to these conversations between various speakers in different situations. Focus on the phrase of certainty or uncertainty in bold in each conversation. What is the speaker trying to say? Circle one of the given choices.

Listening file: Unit_2_Part_2_Activity_1A.mp3

Conversations	Meaning of the phrase
1. Bob left the room and slammed the door behind him. His roommates were surprised: A: What's with him? B: **I think** he is kind of upset.	a. He is upset. b. I am not sure what's going on. c. He may be upset.
2. I ran my bike into a tree. A woman tried to help me get up. She was concerned: A: Are you sure you'll be alright? B: **I guess** so.	a. I am sure. b. I am not sure, but it's OK. c. I am alright.
3. Jim did not show up at the weekly book club meeting. His friends were worried: A: Not sure what happened to Jim. He's never late. B: **I bet** he's sick.	a. He is sick. b. Perhaps he is sick. c. He must be sick.
4. James came out of the staff meeting very disappointed. We were surprised: A: What's going on? B: **I don't know**, but I am so ready to quit!	a. I couldn't care less. b. I really cannot understand it. c. That's crazy!
5. Jane had to study for the finals and take care of her family alone. Her friend tried to comfort her: A: You cannot imagine what I'm going through! B: **I know**, it's hard.	a. I understand. b. I don't know. c. This happened to me, too.

B **LISTEN AND CHECK –** Listen again and verify your guess. Did you guess right?

Listening file: Unit_2_Part_2_Activity_1A.mp3

C **PRACTICE –** Choose the appropriate expression of certainty/uncertainty from the list below to complete each of the following conversations:

I think	**I guess**
I don't know	**I bet**
I know	

1. A: Are you feeling a bit better?
   B: ______________________. It'll take some time . . .
2. A: Sorry, I tried.
   B: ______________________. Don't worry about it.
3. A: I'm looking for Ben.
   B: ______________________ he just left for the day.
4. A: ______________________ you'll never guess what happened to me last week!
   B: What happened?
5. A: It's going to be spring before you know it.
   B: ______________________. This winter seems to be going on forever . . .

Activity 2: Expressing Opinions Through Reaction Phrases

A REVIEW – In the previous unit, we learned several reaction phrases to express evaluation. Some of them are also used to react to opinions. Can you recall any? List them below. (Some are already given.) Share them with your partner and improve your list.

1.		**6.**	
2.		**7.**	**Absolutely.**
3.	**Yeah, that's great!**	**8.**	
4.		**9.**	
5.		**10.**	

B MATCH – Write a reaction phrase you would use to match your classmates' opinions on the left. Use your list of reaction phrases if necessary. The first one is done for you.

Classmates' opinions	Your reaction phrase
1. I'm afraid I am not good at zumba.	a. So what! You can at least try!
2. Gas is so expensive! I think I'll get a bike.	b.
3. This new hairstyle is kind of fun.	c.
4. It looks like it's going to snow again . . .	d.
5. Getting a degree is a lot of work.	e.
6. I've had enough of this weather!	f.
7. Don't you love the new cell design!	g.
8. You rock!	h.

Activity 3 Expressing Degrees of Agreement

A **CATEGORIZE –** When responding to an opinion favorably, people may choose to express agreement at various degrees. Group three of the phrases below under each column according to the degree of agreement they express. Examples are given for each category.

1. I see what you mean.
2. You're absolutely right.
3. Yeah, I can see that.
4. Fair enough.
5. I may have to agree.
6. That's so true.
7. Exactly!
8. I see what you're saying.
9. It could be.

General agreement	Total agreement	Partial disagreement
I see your point.	I totally agree.	I suppose so.

B **FORMULATE OPINIONS –** Read your notes from the preliminary project discussion in your group. Write down three final opinions you have about project options. Follow the given example.

Opinions on the School/Community Development Project

Example: I believe a small sports playground is really useful.

1. ______________________________.
2. ______________________________.
3. ______________________________.

C **SHARE AND REACT –** Share your opinions with your project group. Practice expressing agreement to various degrees to the other group members' opinions. List three of the shared opinions and write an example of agreement to each of them.

Opinions on the School/Community Development Project	Agreement
Example: A small sports playground could be really useful.	Example: Absolutely!
1. ______________	______________.
2. ______________	______________.
3. ______________	______________.

Activity 4: Expressing Degrees of Disagreement

A IDENTIFY – Read the phrases in the table opposite. They signal a different opinion, most probably a disagreement of a certain degree. With a partner, decide on the degree of disagreement of each phrase and check (✓) the appropriate column. Some examples are given.

Disagreement phrase	Acknowledgment and disagreement	Strong disagreement
I see your point but . . .		
Well, yes, but in fact . . .		
That's absolutely ridiculous!		✓
Actually, I find it . . .		
To be honest, I . . .		
You can't be serious!		
Don't be silly!		
You must be kidding me!		
Maybe, but . . .		
True, but I guess . . .	✓	
I see what you mean, but . . .		
That's not funny!		
I'm sorry, but this does not . . .		
I would have to disagree with . . .		

B **MATCH –** Express disagreement appropriately to match each of the situations below. Use phrases from the table above. (Hint: You can soften the expression of disagreement by using an *acknowledgment phrase* first, or other *softening phrases* like "maybe," "I suppose," "It could be . . ."). The first one is done for you.

Situation	Disagreement
1. Your boss asks you to work on the weekend but you have plans already.	**I suppose I could**, but I was hoping to visit my parents in Chicago over the weekend.
2. Your mother believes that you should wear red more often.	
3. Your friend says you should sell your car and buy a bike.	
4. Your father wants you to become a businessman.	
5. Your roommate thinks you spend too much time watching TV.	
6. Your teacher claims that you have missed three classes, when actually you have only missed one.	
7. Your friends tell you that you have to buy them all a meal for your birthday.	

C **PRACTICE –** Role-play three of these situations with your partner. Take turns.

Activity 5: Project Group Discussion

DISCUSS – Work with your group on the project proposal. Use the guiding questions below to prepare your proposal. Make sure that each group member participates actively by exchanging opinions appropriately at least three times. Video-record your group discussion.

Guiding project proposal questions

1. What is the purpose of your project?
2. Who are the project participants?
3. What are the project development stages?
4. What is a possible project cost breakdown? (Detail how much money for which activity)
5. What are some of the project advantages?
6. What are some possible challenges the project may run into?

PART 3: Making and responding to a suggestion/recommendation

Activity 1: Making Suggestions – Focus on Appropriateness

A LISTEN AND ANALYZE – Listen to these short conversations. Focus on the inappropriate suggestions in bold in each of them. Why are they inappropriate? Discuss in your group.

Listening file: Unit_2_Part_3_Activity_1A.mp3

1. (Two friends)

   A: I'm moving to a new apartment. **You have to help me!**

   B: Sure.

2. (A's roommate doesn't look like he wants to go to the movies)

   A: **It would be best if you join me at the movies.**

   B: I'm afraid I have a lot of work to do. Thanks, anyway.

3. (At a party)

   Host: **You must eat more. Here, try this!**

   Guest: Thanks! I am so full . . .

4. (Two classmates)

   A: I did not finish the assignment last night.

   B: **You should make more time**.

5. (Between friends)

   A: Wow, these cookies are so good, but I'm full.

   B: **Yeah, you had better stop eating cookies and go to the gym.**

6. (Student and teacher)

   A: OK, class, the quiz is over. Put your pencils down.

   B: **You've got to give us more time.**

B REWRITE – With your partner, rewrite each inappropriate suggestion.

1. ______________________________.
2. ______________________________.
3. ______________________________.
4. ______________________________.
5. ______________________________.
6. ______________________________.

Activity 2: What Would You Suggest/Recommend?

Ⓐ **MATCH –** Read the following responses. Write down an appropriate suggestion/ recommendation you can make to a friend or colleague to match each response. The first one is done for you.

Suggestion/Recommendation	Response
Have you thought of checking with your landlord first before you get a pet?	Yeah, I might need to.
	Thanks. That's a thought!
	Yeah, maybe you're right.
	I might have to, I guess.
	Really? You think so?
	Nah. I'm alright.
	What do you mean?
	Yeah, I see.

B REWRITE – Now look at the list of phrases to make a suggestion/recommendation. Can you use them to make any of the above suggestions/recommendations better? If "yes," rewrite that suggestion/recommendation.

If I were you . . .

I would . . .

You should . . .

I think you should . . .

I am afraid you might have to . . .

You might want to . . .

Have you thought of . . . ?

Here is a thought: . . .

Why don't you . . . ?

How would you feel about . . . ?

You'd be better off if . . .

Activity 3: Dealing with "Sticky" Problems

PRACTICE – Think of a problem that you might have encountered (it does not have to be true). Write it down on a post-it note and stick it on your sleeve. Go around the classroom and talk to at least six students who are "wearing" their "problem," too. Make and respond to suggestions/recommendations to deal with the problems using the expressions above.

Activity 4: Peer Evaluation

A LISTEN AND EVALUATE – Listen to the recording of a project proposal discussion by another group as assigned by the teacher. Take notes. To evaluate their group communication, think about and respond to the following in writing:

Group you evaluated: ______________________

Group project chosen: ______________________

- Is communication in this group natural?
- Are students facing any communication challenges (e.g., reluctance to talk, going off-task, rambling, etc.)? Give examples.
- Do students respect one another's turn (e.g., turns are taken seamlessly; there are few inappropriate interruptions)?
- Do students use appropriate language to give and react to opinions? If "yes," give an example.
- Do students express agreement/disagreement appropriately? If "yes," give an example.
- Do students exchange any suggestions/recommendations? If "yes," give an example.

B GIVE FEEDBACK – Overall, what was effective and appropriate in this group's communication? What can they improve? Write this information below. Then, share it with the group members whose discussion you evaluated.

Examples of appropriate and effective communication

1. ______________________.
2. ______________________.

Suggestions/recommendations for improvement

1. ______________________.
2. ______________________.

UNIT 2
FINAL UNIT TASK

A PRESENT – In groups of three, present your School/Community Development proposal in class. Prepare to respond to possible suggestions/recommendations for your group project proposal improvement.

B EVALUATE – Your group project proposal and its presentation will be evaluated by the class according to the criteria given below. A "secret" ballot will be cast to decide on the best project proposal.

Performance evaluation criteria	Comments	Points
1. The proposal addressed all the project proposal guiding questions on the project: Purpose Participants Development stages Cost breakdown Advantages Challenges		/6
2. Group members contributed equally to the presentation		/5
3. Group members used appropriate language to express agreement or disagreement with the audience		/3

(Table continued overleaf)

Performance evaluation criteria	Comments	Points
4. Group members used appropriate language to respond to the recommendations made by the audience		/3
5. The proposal was presented fluently and coherently		/4
6. The proposal was accurately and clearly communicated by using correct grammar and pronunciation		/4
Total		**/25**

I would like to improve:

1. ______________________________

2. ______________________________

UNIT 2 SELF-ASSESSMENT: What Progress Did I Make?

1 Review Unit 2 vocabulary list and complete the table below.

	Expressions I can actively use	Expressions I need to review
Part 1 Manage group communication		
Part 2: Express and react to an opinion		
Part 3: Make and respond to a suggestion/recommendation		

II These are the conversation strategies you practiced in this unit. Check (✓) the box in the category that best evaluates your ability to use them.

Strategy	**Very well**	**Fairly well**	**Not very well**
I can interact in a group	☐	☐	☐
I can express an opinion	☐	☐	☐
I can react to an opinion	☐	☐	☐
I can express agreement	☐	☐	☐
I can express disagreement	☐	☐	☐
I can make a suggestion/recommendation	☐	☐	☐
I can respond to a suggestion/recommendation	☐	☐	☐

III Write about what you learned in this unit, and what you plan to continue to work on:

One new skill/strategy I learned in this unit is:

____

____

What I plan to continue to work on is:

____

____

UNIT 2
VOCABULARY LIST

Use the chart below to study the new unit vocabulary and record any new topic-related vocabulary from this unit and elsewhere.

Topic/Function	Vocabulary to review	New vocabulary
Expressions of certainty/ uncertainty	I think I don't know I know I guess	I bet
Expressions of agreement	**General agreement** I see your point. I see what you mean. I see what you're saying. Yeah, I can see that. Right. OK. **Total agreement** I totally agree. You're absolutely right. That's so true. Exactly! Absolutely!	**Agreement with an unfavorable opinion** Actually, I agree. Actually, I don't like it either. To be honest, I hate it, too! I must say, I just can't agree with that. **Partial agreement** I suppose so. I suppose not. Fair enough. It could be.

Topic/Function	Vocabulary to review	New vocabulary
Expressions of disagreement	**Acknowledgment and disagreement** To be honest, I . . . Well, yes, but in fact . . . Actually, I find it . . . I see your point, but . . . True, but I guess . . . I see what you mean, but . . .	**Total disagreement** You can't be serious! You're kidding! That's not funny! **Other expressions of disagreement** I'm sorry, but this does not . . . I would have to disagree with . . .
Expressions to make a suggestion/ recommendation	If I were you . . . I would . . . You should . . . I think you should . . . Have you thought of . . . ? Why don't you . . . ? What about . . . ?	I am afraid you might have to . . . You might want to . . . Here is a thought/ an idea/a suggestion: . . . How would you feel about . . . ? You might be better off if . . .
Expressions to respond to a suggestion/ recommendation	Absolutely! Yeah, I might need to. Really? You think so? Yeah, maybe you're right. Yeah, I see.	Thanks, that's a thought! I might have to, I guess. Nah. I'm alright. What do you mean? So what?

UNIT 2
QUIZ

Activity 1

Listen and complete the student group conversation extracts below. Student A's statement should match Student B's response.

Listening file: Unit_2_Quiz_1.mp3

1.	(Student A alerts the group that they are running short of time) **A:** **B:** Oops, you're right. It's almost time to report.	**3.**	(Student A encourages the group to get back on task) **A:** **B:** OK, sorry.
2.	(Student A checks if his group members got his point) **A:** **B:** To be honest, I'm not sure.	**4.**	(Students are talking all at the same time. Student A helps student B to take her turn) **A:** **B:** I was saying that we might want to decide who does what at some point.

Activity 2

Listen to the following students' opinions about school. Choose the right phrase to express agreement to each of them.

Listening file: Unit_2_Quiz_2.mp3

1.	**A:** The test was not too hard. **B:** a. Yes, it wasn't. b. I could not agree more. c. No, not really.	**3.**	**A:** The workshop was kind of long. **B:** a. Fair enough. b. Yeah, I thought so, too. c. I think yes.
2.	**A:** I really like his teaching style. **B:** a. So do I. b. I see your point. c. To be honest, I like it.	**4.**	**A:** What a lecture . . . Was that boring or what! **B:** a. That's a good point. b. Were you really boring? c. Tell me about it!

Activity 3

Listen to the following opinions exchanged between friends. Write down an appropriate expression of disagreement to react to each of them. Use each expression only one time.

Listening file: Unit_2_Quiz_3.mp3

Opinion	Disagreement
I'm afraid I'm not good at singing.	
This program seems too challenging for me.	
This project is too much work.	
Do they have to play this kind of music all the time?	
If I have to do it all by myself, I give up.	
The new movie was too dramatic for me.	

Activity 4

Match each suggestion/recommendation with the appropriate response. *There is one extra response.*

	Suggestion/Recommendation	Response
1.	I would not push him. He doesn't seem very interested in a new relationship. _____	**a.** Yeah, that's true.
2.	Have you thought of steaming the veggies instead of boiling them? _____	**b.** That's something.
3.	You'd be better off flying to New York. The train takes too long. _____	**c.** Nah, I'll be alright in a few days.
4.	I think you should see a doctor. _____	**d.** Thanks, but I've already been there.
5.	Why don't you come with me to Chicago? _____	**e.** Never, but that's a thought!
6.		**f.** What do you mean?

UNIT 3: EXPRESSING YOURSELF

IN THIS UNIT, YOU WILL LEARN TO:

- **PART 1:** Express and respond to positive feelings
- **PART 2:** Express and respond to negative feelings
- **PART 3:** Talk about feelings

Final Unit Task: In groups, write and record role-playing an "emotional" 2–3-minute mini-movie of a genre of your choice (such as drama, thriller, comedy).

PART 1: Expressing and responding to positive feelings

Activity 1: Let's Get Started

DISCUSS – Read the following statements about happiness, love, and compassion. What do they mean? Do you agree with them? Discuss them in groups.

1. "The best way to cheer yourself up is to cheer somebody else up." Mark Twain
2. "Most folks are as happy as they make up their minds to be." Abraham Lincoln
3. "Compassion is a verb." Thich Nhat Hanh
4. "If you truly loved yourself you could never hurt another." Buddha
5. "Let us always meet each other with smile, for the smile is the beginning of love." Mother Teresa
6. "There is only one happiness in this life: to love and be loved." George Sand.

Activity 2: Let's Review: Expressions of Joy and Enthusiasm

A **LISTEN AND COMPLETE –** Students are sharing exciting news. How do they respond to the news? Listen and complete each response turn with the expression of surprise, joy, or enthusiasm that you hear.

Listening file: Unit_3_Part_1_Activity_2A.mp3

Conversation 1

A: Did I tell you? I got a summer internship in Chicago!

B: ______________________________

Conversation 2

A: I'll be travelling to Tokyo to attend a conference next month. My first time in Japan!

B: ____

Conversation 3

A: I finally got a new laptop. Do you want to see it?

B: ____

Conversation 4

A: Guess what! I got admission in the PhD program in business at this university!

B: ____

Conversation 5

A: Did I tell you that I'm volunteering to build a new community center?

B: ____

Conversation 6

A: I got a free ticket for the game.

B: ____

Conversation 7

A: I didn't get a chance to tell you, but I finally got the new visa.

B: ____

B RESPOND – How would you respond to the news? Listen again and write down your response in the spaces below the box. You can use any of the expressions of joy and enthusiasm in the box. Share your responses with your partner.

Listening file: Unit_3_Part_1_Activity_2B.mp3

That's good news!	I'm thrilled (for you).
Isn't that exciting!	I'm delighted to hear that.
(That's) great!	Congratulations.
(That's) excellent!	I'm so proud of you.
(That's) amazing!	Well done.
(That's) perfect!	Way to go.
Super.	You made it.
Cool.	Hallelujah!
Sweet.	Yippee!
Nice!	Yippee!

Conversation 1

A: Did I tell you? I got a summer internship in Chicago!

Your response: ______________________________

Conversation 2

A: I'll be travelling to Tokyo to attend a conference next month. My first time in Japan!

Your response: ______________________________

Conversation 3

A: I finally got a new laptop. Do you want to see it?

Your response: ______________________________

Conversation 4

A: Guess what! I got admission in the PhD program in business at this university!

Your response: ____________________

Conversation 5

A: Did I tell you that I'm volunteering to build a new community center?

Your response: ____________________

Conversation 6

A: I got a free ticket for the game.

Your response: ____________________

Conversation 7

A: I didn't get a chance to tell you, but I finally got the new visa.

Your response: ____________________

Activity 3: Expressing Empathy

A DISCUSS – When others are feeling bad, we are expected to express empathy. This means that we try to show we understand what they are feeling because we've previously had such an experience, or we can clearly imagine it.

Read and discuss the following questions in your group:

1. How do you express empathy in your culture (for example, by using special language, gestures, rituals, and so on)?
2. What do you say to express and respond to empathy in English? Give an example.

B LISTEN AND IDENTIFY – Jenny has just returned from a conference abroad. She and her friends are chatting at the gym.

Listen to the story Jenny shares with them. Number the expressions of empathy in the order you hear them. Not all the expressions will be used. The first empathy expression ("Oh, I'm so sorry") is marked.

Listening file: Unit_3_Part_1_Activity_3B.mp3

Order	Expressions of empathy
	You must have been really stressed out.
	I would have been devastated!
	What a shame.
1	Oh, I'm so sorry.
	I'm so happy for you, Jenny!
	I hear you.
	That's a pain, isn't it?
	That's frustrating.
	Oh, no wonder!
	That's horrible.
	That's too bad.
	I can imagine how you must have felt.

C PRACTICE – Get into groups of three students. Pick a story slip from an envelope of mini stories given by the teacher and share it with your group members. They should react to the story and express empathy by using appropriate expressions. Take turns.

Activity 4: Expressing Sympathy and Sorrow

A **LISTEN AND IDENTIFY** – Listen to the expressions of sympathy and sorrow in the table below. While listening, check (✓) the ones you have heard or used before. Complete the table with an example of a situation each expression can be used in. (Note: Some expressions can be used in multiple situations.)

Listening file: Unit_3_Part_1_Activity_4A.mp3

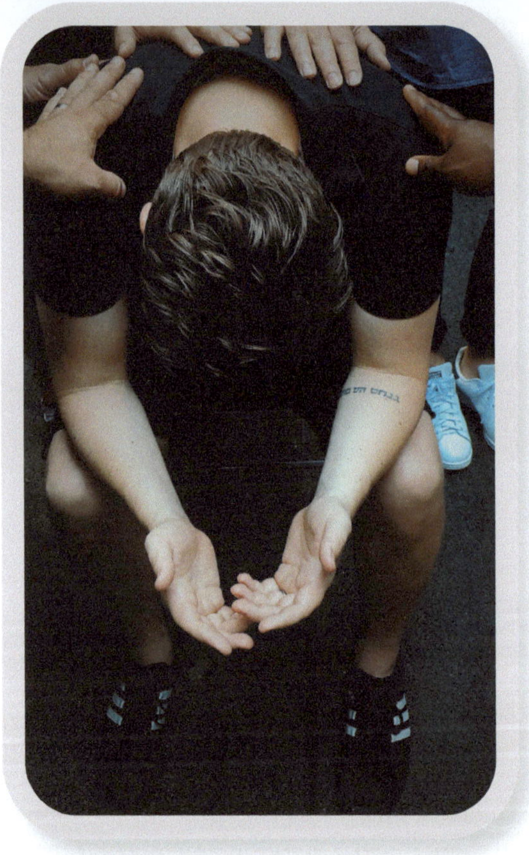

I have used/ heard this before	Expression of sympathy and sorrow	Situation
	I am so sorry about it.	
	I will be thinking of you.	
	I'm so sad to hear about . . .	
	I heard about . . . and I am extremely sorry.	
	My condolences.	
	I heard what happened. My deepest sympathy.	
	I can't believe that happened to you.	
✓	I hope you get better soon.	To wish someone sick a quick recovery
	I want you to know that I'm here for you.	
	Sorry you are going through this.	

B **COMPLETE AND PRACTICE** – Read the following responses. Under what circumstance would you respond that way? Discuss with a partner. Write down an expression of sympathy or sorrow to match each of them. Then take turns to practice the mini-conversations together. The first one is done for you.

Conversation 1

A: I am so terribly sorry for what you are going through.

B: Thank you very much. I appreciate it.

Conversation 2

A: ____

B: Thank you, but please don't worry. I'll be fine.

Conversation 3

A: ____

B: Thank you. It's hard, but we are working through it.

Conversation 4

A: ____

B: Thanks for your support.

Conversation 5

A: ____

B: That's very thoughtful of you. Thank you!

Conversation 6

A: ____

B: Thank you. You're very kind, but we'll manage.

C LISTEN AND MATCH – As we have seen in this unit, the expression "I'm sorry" (used to apologize) often indicates empathy, sympathy, regret, and other, depending on the context. A helpful way to identify its meaning is to identify the context and listen to the intonation this expression is spoken with.

Listen to the following conversations made in various situations. Match the meaning of "Sorry" or "I'm sorry" with each situation. Share with your partner. One match is done for you.

Listening file: Unit_3_Part_1_Activity_4C.mp3

	Situation	Meaning of "I'm sorry"
1. __	**A:** Excuse me. **B:** I'm sorry. (Moves away from the bus door)	a. Can you say it again, please?
2. __	**A:** I'm so sorry. I missed the bus. **B:** You're good. It's just 5:01.	b. I feel bad for you.
3. __	**A:** You need to pay the library fine before you can borrow another book. **B:** I'm sorry?	c. Please accept my sympathy for her death.
4. __	**A:** My cat died over the weekend. **B:** I'm really sorry. I know how much you loved her.	d. I apologize.
5. __	**A:** Sorry, is this seat taken? **B:** No, I don't think so.	e. I can see that, but I'm not taking my comment back.
6. __	**A:** I have a terrible headache. **B:** I'm sorry.	f. Who, me? You must be wrong.
7. _e_	**A:** That's a terrible thing to say. **B:** I'm sorry you feel that way.	g. Excuse me.
8. __	**A:** I'm sorry? **B:** At 8am, not 9am.	h. I apologize for blocking the way.

PART 2:
Expressing and responding to negative feelings

Activity 1: How Well Do You Manage Anger?

A COMPLETE – Answer the following survey questions about anger:

Questions	Not true	Sometimes true	Often true
1. I do not get angry very easily.			
2. When I am angry, I try to control myself.			
3 When I am angry, I avoid "snapping back" at the person who made me angry.			
4. I try to talk to the person who made me angry when I have calmed down.			
5. I like to talk to a close friend about the event that caused anger.			
6. I try not to think too hard about what happened.			
7. I try to work out in the gym to forget the anger episode.			
8. I forgive the person who made me angry.			
9. I avoid situations that make me angry.			
10. I avoid discussing hot topics with people who get angry easily.			

SCORE INTERPRETATION

Not true – More than 5: You need to learn a lot how to manage your anger and not let it mess up your emotional life.
Sometimes true – More than 5: You can control your anger sometimes but not always. Keep learning about yourself, what makes you angry, and how to curb it.
Often true – More than 5: You know what to do to manage your anger.

B COMPARE AND DISCUSS – What did you find out about yourself? Share your survey results with your partner.

Activity 2: Expressing Anger

A DISCUSS – Think about the following questions. Share your answers in your group.

1. What do you do when other people are angry or annoyed (not necessarily because of you)?
2. From your experience, what works best to control these negative emotions?

B LISTEN AND DISCUSS – At a school dorm, two students are talking about their roommate. Listen and answer the following questions. Discuss your answers with your partner.

Listening file: Unit_3_Part_2_Activity_2B.mp3

1. Why is Karen upset? Explain her reasons.
2. How does she express her negative feelings? Identify at least three expressions of anger.
3. How does Chris handle this situation? Identify and discuss at least two strategies she uses to address Karen's anger.

Activity 3: What Upsets You?

A COMPLETE – Complete the following statements about what makes you upset. Share them with your partner. The first one is done for you.

1. It really bothers me *when you play loud music when I am studying.*
2. I can't stand it when ____.
3. It drives me crazy when ______________________________________.
4. It annoys me when ____.
5. I can't take it when ____.
6. It kills me when ____.
7. I can't believe it when ______________________________________.
8. It drives me up the wall when _________________________________.

B RESPOND AND ADVISE – Use the following expressions to advise your partner how he/she can handle five of the irritating situations above.

If I were you . . .	I would/wouldn't . . .
Why don't you try to . . . ?	Have you tried . . . ?
What if you tried . . . ?	Have you thought of . . . ?
I think you should/shouldn't . . .	You could . . .
It might help you if you . . .	

For example:

A: It drives me crazy when my brother uses my computer without my permission.
B: **I think you should** change the log-in information.

DID YOU KNOW THAT . . . ?

Listening file: Unit_3_Part_2_Activity_3_box.mp3

English language has its own "melody": that is, loudness varies and voice rises and falls according to typical patterns, despite user variation. These patterns are important to understand the speaker's attitude and purpose, and the meaning of the phrase.

When we express strong feelings such as excitement, joy, anger, and so on, we are generally loud. In contrast, we sound less loud when we express feelings such as boredom, lack of interest, uncertainty, and others.

The rising and falling intonation patterns when we express feelings vary, too. Generally, in exclamations (outbursts of positive or negative emotions), the voice goes down at the end of the word/phrase. Surprise, joy or enthusiasm, anger, empathy, and so on, fall into this category.

For example:

Surprise	**Unbelievable ↘**
	You're kidding. ↘
Joy/Enthusiasm	**Excellent! ↘**
	Way to go! ↘
Anger	**Stop it! ↘**
	What a pain. ↘
Empathy	**I'm so sorry.↘**
	That's terrible. ↘

However, when we show interest (that is, "Can you tell me more?"), the voice rises:

Oh! ↗
Oh really? ↗
Is that right? ↗
You're moving? ↗

It is important to recognize these patterns and practice them in your own speech so that you improve your chances of being better understood in English.

Activity 4: Expressing Your Feelings

PRACTICE – Complete the following conversation between two students with expressions that indicate feelings. Then, practice reading it with your partner. Take turns.

Ben: What's up? You look tired.

Jim: Oh yeah. It's been quite a week.

Ben: What's going on?

Jim: I had a car accident and totaled my car.

Ben: ____ (Express surprise and empathy) What happened?

Jim: I don't know. The car broke down in the highway. To think that I had just had a car check-up! ____________________________________ (Expresses anger)

Ben: ________________________ (Express empathy). Can't you fix the car at all?

Jim: Well, I can, but it costs less to buy a used car.

Ben: ________________________ (Express anger and empathy)

So, what do you do to get to class? You still live out of town, right?

Jim: Yeah. Well, I had to buy another car.

Ben: ________________________ (Expresses surprise). Well, I know it stretches your budget but ________________________ (Expresses excitement).

Jim: Thanks, Ben! I hope it's worth it.

PART 3:
Talking about feelings

Activity 1: Describing Degrees of Feelings

A SEARCH – When we describe feelings in English we often use intensifiers to indicate their degree and intensity. Intensifier + descriptive adjectives are very high-frequency collocations in spoken English. Let's search for the most frequent intensifiers that go with adjectives very commonly used to describe personal feelings in this genre. Work in pairs.

1. Log in to the Corpus of Contemporary American English (COCA).
2. In the SEARCH box, choose the LIST setting, then type [r*] which stands for adverbs, and the high-frequency descriptive adjective as assigned by the teacher.

For example:

[r*] disappointed

3. Click on 'Sections', and then click next on the word 'SPOKEN' from the list of options in list 1 (see the screenshot).
4. Click on 'Find matching strings'.
5. Pick the top five most typical intensifiers the adjective is used with. Enter this information in the table on the next page.

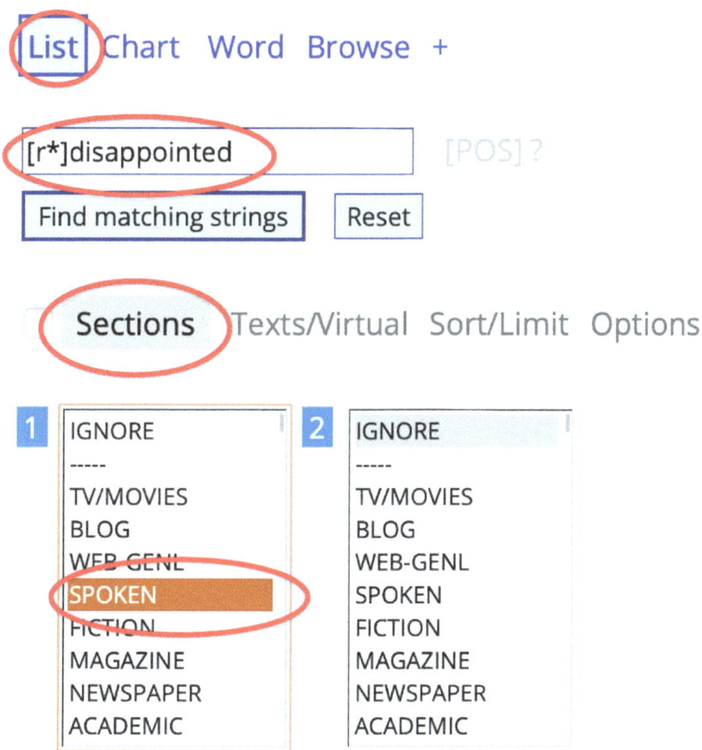

6. Enter ONE example of the most frequent intensifier + adjective use. To do this, click on an entry in the Chart view (such as 'VERY DISAPPOINTED'). This will bring up a set of concordance lines from the 'Spoken' section of COCA.

The first example is done for you.

Top five most frequent intensifiers	Frequent adjectives descriptive of personal feelings	Corpus example from spoken English
very; little; so; deeply; really	**Disappointed**	I was very, **very disappointed,** and it hurt to watch.
	Excited	
	Thrilled	
	Happy	
	Optimistic	
	Upset	
	Worried	
	Shocked	
	Outraged	

B **PRACTICE –** Think of two situations when you felt the way described by the adjectives in the table above. Take turns and share each situation with your partner, using at least two of these adjectives and their intensifiers.

Activity 2 Phrasal Verbs of Feelings

Phrasal verbs are very commonly used in informal spoken English and they add color and richness to the language. In particular, the use of phrasal verbs to indicate feelings enhances their intensity and adds drama to the oral interaction.

A MATCH – Match the phrasal verbs of feelings with their meanings. Share your choices with your partner. The first one is done for you.

Answer	Phrasal verb	Meaning
1. _d__	**Cheer up**	a. Annoy or upset someone by persistent action
2. ___	Calm down	b. Stop it
3. ___	Be carried away	c. Stop feeling angry, upset, or overexcited
4. ___	Go easy on	**d. Feel happier**
5. ___	Cut it out	e. Calm down after being agitated
6. ___	Tick somebody off	f. Make somebody annoyed or angry
7. ___	Be fed up with	g. Be overexcited about something and behave in a hasty or unreasonable way
8. ___	Get over	h. Upset someone greatly
9. ___	Freak out	i. Try to forget about an unpleasant event or behavior
10.___	Tear someone apart	j. Cannot stand someone's behavior
11. ___	Get to someone	k. Refrain from being harsh or too critical
12. ___	Cool off	l. Behave in a strange and violent way

B FILL IN THE BLANKS – Use the phrasal verbs in the table above to complete the following conversations. Share your choices with your partner. The first one is done for you.

Conversation 1

A: I really love learning Japanese, but I have not had a second to study it these days. Finishing up the dissertation is such a pain! I am so __ **fed up**________________ with it.

B: Hey, ___________! It's almost over. And, didn't you tell me that you are traveling to Japan for Christmas? Isn't that awesome to practice the language?

Conversation 2

A. This new chapter in math is pretty tough. The quiz is this Monday, right? I'm so ______ out.

B. Don't let it ________you. I'm sure you'll feel much better once you have some more time to study over the weekend.

Conversation 3

A: Hey, Mom, ______! I'm back!

B: Thank goodness! The thought that you could have had an accident on the way was ______.

Conversation 4

A: Sorry, I was so ______________with the idea that we can finally enjoy the Break! I totally forgot about the take-home exam we planned to work on together. I am so sorry. Is it possible to reschedule the study group meeting?

B: Not to worry, we sure can. By the way, the idea that we have to finish two take-home exams during the Spring Break was ____________, too. How cruel is that?

Activity 3: Feelings Through Idiomatic Expressions

Spoken English abounds in colorful idiomatic expressions that indicate feelings. Just like the phrasal verbs of emotions, they make our oral expression more natural, fluent, and richer.

A **ACT THEM OUT** – Work in pairs and look up the meaning of the two assigned idioms from the list below. Then, take turns and act them out silently in front of the class. Give non-verbal hints until the class finds out the idiom you are describing. Explain the meaning and usage of the idiom in English.

Idiom of feelings	Meaning	Example
1. On cloud nine	Extremely happy	She was on cloud nine when she got married.
2. On top of the world		
3. Sick and tired of		
4. Breathe down somebody's neck		
5. Drive somebody up the wall		
6. Get on somebody's nerves		
7. Rub somebody the wrong way		
8. Take it easy		

B **DESCRIBE** – In pairs, use the factual information below and write a colorful story in 7–8 sentences about your first trip abroad. The story can be real or fictional. Make sure you use four idioms indicating feelings. Share your story in class.

The facts

1. You were very happy to travel but were scared of flying.
2. The flight was hard.
3. The person next to you was snoring all the time.
4. The flight attendant was slow.
5. The line at the passport control point was very long.
6. You were so relieved when you got your luggage.
7. Finally, you met your friends at the airport.

UNIT 3
FINAL UNIT TASK

A **WRITE AND RECORD** – In groups of three students, write and record role-playing an "emotional" 2-3-minute mini-movie of a genre of your choice (such as drama, thriller, comedy).

When you prepare this task, make sure that you:

a. express and respond to feelings appropriately
b. use intensifiers to show various degrees of feelings
c. create colorful, dramatic effects by using phrasal verbs and idioms of feeling
d. use appropriate intonation when expressing and responding to feelings
e. participate in the role-play equally and actively.

You can prepare a mini-movie script based on:

1. A real-life story
2. An impressive short story
3. A memorable movie scene
4. A TV show or sitcom
5. A new story you write as a group

B EVALUATE – Watch another group's mini-movie, as assigned by the teacher. Use the following rubric to evaluate their performance. Get together with the other group and discuss your evaluation. Your group's performance will be evaluated and discussed in the same way.

Performance evaluation criteria	Comments	Points
Group:		
1. Developed the mini-movie sufficiently		/3
2. Expressed and responded to feelings (positive and/or negative) properly at least three times		/6
3. Used intensifiers at least two times (e.g., **so** thrilled; **really** happy)		/2
4. Used phrasal verbs of feelings at least two times (e.g., tick off; get to)		/2
5. Used at least two idioms of feeling (e.g., drive somebody crazy; tickled pink)		/2
6. Worked collaboratively and participated equally		/2
Student:		
1. Participated actively in the role-play		/2
2. Talked naturally (avoiding many non-native pauses)		/2
3. Used intonation to express feelings effectively		/2
4. Used correct grammar to accomplish the task with minimal errors that did not prevent communication		/2
Total		**/25**

I would like to improve:

1. ______________________________

2. ______________________________

UNIT 3 SELF-ASSESSMENT: What Progress Did I Make?

1 Review Unit 3 vocabulary list and complete the table below.

	Expressions I can actively use	Expressions I need to review
Part 1: Express and respond to positive feelings		
Part 2: Express and respond to negative feelings		
Part 3: Talk about feelings		

II These are the conversation strategies you practiced in this unit. Check (✓) the box in the category that best evaluates your ability to use them.

Strategy	Very well	Fairly well	Not very well
I can express and respond to joy and excitement	☐	☐	☐
I can express and respond to empathy	☐	☐	☐
I can express and respond to sympathy and sorrow	☐	☐	☐
I can express and respond to anger and annoyance	☐	☐	☐
I can express feelings with appropriate intonation	☐	☐	☐
I can use intensifiers to express feelings	☐	☐	☐
I can use phrasal verbs to talk about feelings	☐	☐	☐
I can use idioms to talk about feelings	☐	☐	☐

III Write about what you learned in this unit, and what you plan to continue to work on:

One new skill/strategy I learned in this unit is:

____

____

What I plan to continue to work on is:

____

____

UNIT 3
VOCABULARY LIST

Use the chart below to study the new unit vocabulary and record any new topic-related vocabulary from this unit and elsewhere.

Topic/Function	Vocabulary to review	New vocabulary
Expressions of joy and enthusiasm	That's good news! Good for you! Isn't that exciting? (That's) great! (That's) excellent! (That's) amazing! (That's) awesome! Thank God!/goodness! Super. Cool. Sweet. Perfect! Ah/Ahh/Ooh! Nice!	I'm so happy/glad to hear that. Well done. Way to go. You made it. Hallelujah! Yippee! Hooray! Yay! **Phrasal verbs** Cheer up **Idioms** On cloud nine A happy camper On top of the world

(Table continued overleaf)

Topic/Function	Vocabulary to review	New vocabulary
Expressions of empathy, sympathy, and sorrow	I'm so sorry. That's terrible. That sounds horrible. That's too bad. That's frustrating. I know how it feels. Oh, I am so sorry that happened. I'm so sad to hear about . . . I can't believe that happened. Let me know if you need anything. Let me know if there's anything I can do.	I hear you. I feel for you. I share your (frustration/anger/pain/loss). Oh, it's such a shame. I know it is not easy for you, but . . . What an awful situation for you. You must have really been stressed out. I understand what you're going through. I can't imagine how you must be feeling right now. I heard about your loss. My condolences/My deepest sympathy. **Phrasal verbs** Cheer up **Idioms** Hang in there. Go easy on . . . Don't kill yourself over . . .

(Table continued from previous page)

Topic/Function	Vocabulary to review	New vocabulary
Expressions of annoyance and anger	I can't believe this! What a pain. That's so annoying. Stop it! It's none of your business. I don't care. Leave me alone. That's ridiculous! Hey, relax/chill out!	I can't stand it when . . . It drives me crazy/nuts when . . . It annoys me when . . . I can't take it when . . . It kills me when . . . I can't believe it when . . . Watch it, buddy! Cool it! **Phrasal verbs** Piss somebody off (slang) Tick somebody off Be fed up with Tear someone apart **Idioms** Get off my back! Cut it out! That's going too far. Get on somebody's nerves Rub somebody the wrong way Drive somebody up the wall Breathe down somebody's neck Be sick and tired of

(Table continued from previous page)

UNIT 3 QUIZ

Activity 1

Listen and complete the conversation turns below with an appropriate expression of positive evaluation.

Listening file: Unit_3_Quiz_1.mp3

1.	**A:** I'll join the university dancing club next semester. **B:**	**3.**	**A:** I am really happy! I got admitted to the PhD program in computer science. **B:**
2.	**A:** It turns out I do not need to take another stats course for credit. **B:**	**4.**	**A:** So, I finally got to go to the Grand Canyon this summer. **B:**

Activity 2

Listen to the following conversations. Choose the right expression of empathy to react to each of them.

Listening file: Unit_3_Quiz_2.mp3

1.	**A:** Hey, I got your text, but I will not be able to make it. I need to take my dog to the hospital again. The doctor said she may need surgery. **B:** a. Oh, it's such a pain, I understand. b. Oh, I can't believe that happened. c. Oh, I hope she is going to be OK.	**3.**	**A:** So, by the end of the week I have to defend the prelims and move out. **B:** a. Oh, it's such a shame. b. Wow, that's a lot! c. You must have been really stressed out.
2.	**A:** I found out I need three more units to graduate. I was so hoping to finish school this summer . . . **B:** a. Oh, how frustrating. b. Hmm. What a pity. c. Let me know if you need anything.	**4.**	**A:** My bike broke, so I have to walk to school everyday now. It takes forever . . . **B:** a. Really? That's good exercise. b. I can't imagine how you must be feeling right now. c. What a shame.

Activity 3

Listen to the following conversations. Explain the meaning of "I'm sorry" in each of them.

Listening file: Unit_3_Quiz_3.mp3

	Conversation	Meaning of "I'm sorry"
1.	(Two passengers on the bus) **A:** Whoops, I'm sorry. **B:** You're fine.	
2.	(Two strangers chatting on the train) **A:** Are you married? **B.** I'm sorry?	
3.	**A:** Sorry? **B:** I said next Monday.	
4.	**A:** You must be Ben's fiancée. **B:** I'm sorry?	
5.	**A:** I've had a bad cold all week. **B:** I'm sorry.	
6.	**A:** You were a bit too hard on your younger brother. **B:** I'm sorry you feel that way. He needs to be responsible.	

Activity 4

Rewrite the following statements of anger or annoyance by using the appropriate phrasal verb or idiom from the list below. There is one extra choice.

Be fed up with	Drive somebody up the wall
Step on someone's toes	Breathe down somebody's neck
Grate on somebody's nerves	Be sick and tired of

1. Her boss monitors her performance very closely.

____

2. My younger brother annoys me when he leaves dirty dishes in the sink all the time.

____

3. I don't want to clean the room for my roommate anymore.

____

4. His remark about discipline irritated his coworkers.

____

5. I warned her not to get involved in Bob's business, because it's going to upset him a lot.

____

UNIT 4: GETTING THINGS DONE

IN THIS UNIT, YOU WILL LEARN TO:

- **PART 1:** Make and respond to direct requests
- **PART 2:** Make and respond to indirect requests
- **PART 3:** Soften requests

Final Unit Task: Video- or audio-record making and responding to a request appropriately in two situations.

PART 1:
Making and responding to direct requests

Activity 1: Let's Get Started

A LISTEN AND DISCUSS – Listen to the students' requests in the conversations below. Every request is inappropriate. Discuss each conversation with your partner and consider the situation and the speaker–listener relationship.

Listening file: Unit_4_Part_1_Activity_1A.mp3

1. At the end of class

A student has questions about his quiz errors:

Teacher: Would you like to make an appointment to go over the quiz together, then?

Student: Yes. Thank you. Let me visit your office on Wednesday.

2. At the international student advisor's office

A student finds the door open and walks into the international student advisor's office:

Student: Hi, my friend told me that I should see you. I will go to Canada. Can you sign my I-20 now?

Advisor: Well, . . .

3. At the end of the quiz

A student is asking when the quiz will be graded:

Teacher: OK, time is up. Please turn in the quizzes, everybody.

Student: (*handing in the quiz to the teacher*) How about the grades?

4. At the academic advisor's office

A student is inquiring about sources of funding to support his studies:

Academic advisor: Have you thought about applying for a research assistantship?

Student: I am not sure. Can you give me an assistantship for next semester?

B REWRITE – Can you make each request fit the situation and the speaker–listener relationship? Rewrite and share your revised requests in class.

Activity 2: Making Pre-requests

A **ANALYZE –** Sometimes, we want to know whether it is OK to make the request or not. So, we may first ask a question to find out. We call this a "pre-request."

Look at these pre-requests. Who are the people talking to in each situation? What kind of relationship are they in? Analyze the pre-requests and brainstorm potential answers to complete the second and third columns. The first one is done for you.

Pre-request	Who is talking to whom	Relationship (formal/informal)
You got a sec?	**Friends, colleagues**	**Informal**
Can you do me a favor?		
Lisa, would you do me a favor, please?		
Hey, do me a favor . . .		
Sorry, can I bother you for a sec?		
Do you have any plans this weekend?		
I was wondering if I could ask you a favor.		
Are you terribly busy this Saturday?		

B RESPOND – Based on the information in the table above, write down a response to each pre-request. Choose another response if the pre-request does not encourage a request. See the given examples.

	Pre-request	Response to pre-request	Request	Other response (request not possible)
1.	**You got a sec?**	**Sure, what's up?**	**Can you look at this and tell me what you think?**	
2.	Can you do me a favor?			

(Table continued overleaf)

	Pre-request	Response to pre-request	Request	Other response (request not possible)
3.	Lisa, would you do me a favor, please?			
4.	Hey, do me a favor . . .			
5.	**Sorry, can I bother you for a sec?**	**Can you give me a few minutes? I'm finishing up a business email.**		**Sure, no problem!**
6.	Do you have any plans this weekend?			
7.	I was wondering if I could ask you a favor.			
8.	Are you terribly busy this Saturday?			

Activity 3: Responding to Requests

ROLE-PLAY – Choose two of the completed requests in Activity 2B above. With your partner, role-play accepting and declining each of them. Make sure to use appropriate expressions from the table below. Take turns.

NOTE: When you decline a request, you usually:

1. apologize
2. provide reasons for declining
3. offer to make up for it, if possible.

Example:
Request: Can you look at this and tell me what you think?
Declining the request: I am sorry (1), I am afraid this will take me some time to review, and I need to go to the lecture (2). Can I look at this after class today (3)?

Expressions to accept a request	**Expressions to decline a request**
Absolutely.	Sorry, but I . . .
Definitely.	I am sorry, I can't because . . .
Sure.	Well, I wish I could, but . . .
Sure thing.	You see, the thing is . . .
OK.	Well, I hate to say "no" but . . .
No problem.	I would like to (help you), but I can't because . . .
Of course!	I'm afraid I can't because . . .
I would be glad to.	I can't believe I'm saying this, but I'm gonna (going to) have to say "no."
My pleasure.	

Activity 4: Making Face-to-Face Requests

A **LISTEN AND ANALYZE –** Listen to the response to each of the following request situations. Based on the response, are the situations formal or informal? Circle (F) for formal and (I) for informal. The first one is done for you.

Listening file: Unit_4_Part_1_Activity_4A.mp3

1. **You want to borrow your friend's electronic dictionary.** F (I)

   A:

   B. Sure. Here you go.

2. **You need a two-day extension to complete your paper in the Psychology class.** F I

   A:

   B. I normally do not give extensions. Is there a problem?

3. You need to return a sweater in the store. F I

A:

B. Was anything wrong with it?

4. You want to borrow your neighbor's car Saturday evening. F I

A:

B. Well, I hate to say "no" but I'm gonna need it on the weekend. I'm going out of town. Sorry!

5. You need to register for the aerobics class, but the registration deadline was the day before. F I

A:

B. Sorry but the registration deadline has passed, and the class is full.

6. You need to call the doctor, but you discover you left your phone at home. Ask your classmate to lend you his. F I

A:

B. OK. I hope they don't put you on hold for life . . . Just kidding!

7. You want to get coffee at the university library's café. F I

A:

B. For here or to go?

8. **You need a ride to the city airport at noon tomorrow. Ask your new friend to help you with it.** F I

A:

B. Tomorrow? I'm sorry, I'm afraid I can't make it. I just made lunch plans with a friend.

B MATCH AND ROLE-PLAY – Use request examples from the chart below to formulate your request so that it matches each situation and response above. Then role-play three of the situations with your partner.

Expressions to make direct requests

Paper or plastic?

Something to drink?

Can you hand me the manual, please?

Can I use it for a sec?

Could I use your phone, please?

How about meeting at 10am?

10am's OK?

Do you have a quarter I could borrow?

Do you by any chance have any Kleenex?

Is it OK if I keep this book a bit longer?

Do you mind if I sit here?

Would you mind if I borrowed your bike for ten minutes?

Would you be willing to help with it?

I was wondering if I could leave the class early today.

Would you happen to have change for a twenty?

Do you think you could possibly lend me your car until Saturday?

Activity 5: Making Requests on the Phone

A **COMPLETE –** Each of the following phrases signals a request. How would you use them to make a request on the phone? Complete each request. Think of a possible situation when each request can be used appropriately.

Phone request	Possible situation
Example: I would like to talk to Mr. Binder, please.	Example: Calling an office to speak with someone.
1. May I ask you to call . . . ?	1.
2. I was wondering if you could cancel . . .	2.
3. I want to check . . .	3.
4. I need . . .	4.
5. Can you verify . . . ?	5.
6. Do you offer . . . ?	6.
7. Please send . . .	7.
8. Could you tell me . . . ?	8.
9. Would you like me to . . . ?	9.
10. Do you mind if I . . . ?	10.

B LISTEN AND MAKE A REQUEST – You need to request information or a service by phone. Listen to the telephone prompt. Write down a greeting or introduction followed by an appropriate request. Here is an example:

What you hear: Hampton Inn. How can I help you?

What you may say: This is room 305. Can you give me a wake-up call tomorrow at 6am, please?

Listening file: Unit_4_Part_1_Activity_5B.mp3

	Place you are calling	Greeting/Introduction and request
1.	Student health center	**Greeting/Introduction:** **Request:**
2.	Cellular phone company	**Greeting/Introduction:** **Request:**
3.	Apartment management office	**Greeting/Introduction:** **Request:**
4.	Department store	**Greeting/Introduction:** **Request:**
5.	Apartment maintenance	**Greeting/Introduction:** **Request:**
6.	Student services	**Greeting/Introduction:** **Request:**
7.	Flower shop	**Greeting/Introduction:** **Request:**
8.	University library	**Greeting/Introduction:** **Request:**

C **PRACTICE –** Locate the phone information of a business in town you need to call. With your partner, take turns to role-play the phone call and make your request. Record the conversations. Then, discuss the phone interaction and provide feedback on request appropriateness.

PART 2:
Making and responding to indirect requests

Activity 1: Identifying Indirect Requests

A **LISTEN AND ANALYZE –** Students are ordering lunch on a hot summer day. Listen to their conversations. How are requests being made? How do students respond to each of them? Underline all requests and responses. Discuss them with your partner.

Listening file: **Unit_4_Part_2_Activity_1A.mp3**

B LISTEN AND MATCH – Many of the requests in the conversation above are made indirectly. Some are simply personal comments/opinions/complaints that may express a hidden request to do something different.

The indirect requests and their responses in this conversation are scrambled in the table below.

Listen to the conversation again and match each indirect request with its respective response. The first one is done for you.

Indirect request	Response
1. __c__ I'm dying for a freshly squeezed fruit juice. **2.** ____ Oh man, it's so crowded here! **3.** ____ I've been curious about the fig and roasted walnuts one. **4.** ____ Anything that doesn't have capers on it! **5.** ____ I'm really hot. **6.** ____ I love the little Indian place next to the dorm. **7.** ____ We might still have time to go to Gianni's, though. **8.** ____ Oh, boy, look at that big one! **9.** ____ Oh my goodness, I'm going be swept away before I know it! **10.** _____ Sorry, I'm a bit slow today.	**a.** Oh yeah. That's a cute one. **b.** Sure! **c.** Sorry, we only have bottled juices. **d.** Water, lemonade, ice tea? **e.** Yeah. And it's really noisy! **f.** Yeah, that looks interesting. Let's try it! **g.** Yeah, that's humongous! **h.** Yep, you're right! **i.** No problem. I'll give you a few more minutes. **j.** No kidding! There should be a way to turn it down a bit.

Activity 2: Understanding and Responding to Indirect Requests

A **LISTEN AND DISCUSS** – The following conversations begin at a dorm. The speaker is trying to formulate an indirect request in each situation. Listen and discuss each speaker's indirect request statement with your partner.

Listening file: Unit_4_Part_2_Activity_2A.mp3

Scene	Speaker's statement	Meaning
1. Dorm room (when noticing the roommate had not cleaned the room)	Oh my God! This room is a total mess.	
2. Cafeteria (when noticing someone cutting in line)	What! He must be kidding me! (to the person cutting in line): Sorry, the line starts here.	
3. Study room (when entering a non-air-conditioned room	Is it me, or is it this room? I'm kind of hot.	
4. Friend's party (when looking at cookies)	Wow! These cookies look really yummy.	
5. In front of the TV (when bothered by the loud volume of the TV)	Boy, he is loud, isn't he?	

B RESPOND – How would you respond to the indirect request in each situation? Write your responses in the chart below.

Scene	Speaker's statement	Your response
1. Dorm room	Oh my God! This room is a total mess.	
2. Cafeteria	What! He must be kidding me! Sorry, the line starts here.	
3. Study room	Is it me, or is it this room? I'm kind of hot.	
4. Friend's party	Wow! These cookies look really yummy.	
5. In front of the TV	Boy, he is loud, isn't he?	

Activity 3: Making Indirect Requests

REWRITE – Look at the following requests and who they are addressed to. Rewrite only the ones that need to be indirect.

Example:

Direct	**Indirect**
Stop smoking.	Smoking is not allowed in this car.

Direct	**Indirect**
1. (to the secretary) Fix this copy machine.	______________________
2. (to the landlord) Check the air conditioning.	______________________
3. (to a passenger on a train) Can I sit here?	______________________

4. (to your roommate) Clean this room. ____________________
5. (to your friend) Can you help me with moving? ____________________
6. (to your friend, in disbelief) Yeah, right. Give me a break! ____________________
7. (to a classmate) Can you carry these boxes for me? ____________________
8. (to your spouse) Get yourself out of there (the office). It's too late. ____________________
9. (to your sister, who is trying to trick you) Get out! ____________________

PART 3: Softening requests

Activity 1: Understanding the Use of "Please"

Listening file: Unit_4_Part_3_box_1.mp3

DID YOU KNOW THAT . . . ?

We often believe that adding "please" makes a request sound more polite in spoken interaction. Take a look at the following:

1. **Correct my draft, please.**
2. **Send me the homework, please.**
3. **Show me my errors, please.**
4. **Check my statement of purpose, please.**
5. **Show me my attendance, please.**

Why aren't these statements polite? What can they tell you about the listener–speaker relationship they imply?

In fact:

- "Please" is more common in formal writing than in formal speech.
- When "please" occurs in formal speech, it is more often used with requests made on the phone in standard, routinized situations such as:
    1. asking the other person to wait in the line
    2. asking to speak to a special person
    3. asking somebody to call back
    4. leaving a message
    5. asking for an extension, a special department, a telephone number.
- "Could you" has been replacing "please" to show politeness in informal speech.

(Aijmer, K. *Conversational Routines in English: Convention and Creativity*. London and New York: Routledge, 2014)

A ANALYZE AND IDENTIFY – Listen to the request statement in each situation. Who is talking to whom? What is the speaker trying to say or do? Write down the possible meaning of "please" in each statement.

Example:

Request statement	**Meaning of "please"**
Please leave!	Warning.

Request statement	**Meaning of "please"**
1. Oh, please, Jack! For heaven's sake!	______________
2. Diet Coke, please.	______________
3. Next slide, please.	______________
4. Girls, please! Quiet!	______________
5. Yes, please?	______________
6. Would you please . . . (pauses in anger)!	______________

Listening file: Unit_4_Part_3_Activity_1A.mp3

B LISTEN AND DESCRIBE – "Please" in requests can have various intonation patterns, depending on politeness, expectations, the speaker's intent and emotional state. In general, "please" in polite requests has a rising intonation. In an elevated emotional state, "please" can be realized with a falling intonation.

Now, go back to the request statements above. Listen and determine its intonation pattern in each statement:

Listening file: Unit_4_Part_3_Activity_1B.mp3

1. Oh, please, Jack! For heavens' sake!	[Rising]	[Falling]
2. Diet Coke, please.	[Rising]	[Falling]
3. Next slide, please.	[Rising]	[Falling]
4. Girls, please! Quiet!	[Rising]	[Falling]
5. Yes, please?	[Rising]	[Falling]
6. Would you please . . . (pauses in anger)!	[Rising]	[Falling]

C LISTEN AND REPEAT – Listen again to each statement and repeat after the speaker.

Listening file: Unit_4_Part_3_Activity_1C.mp3

Activity 2: Using Hedgers

A DISCUSS – Hedgers are words/phrases which are often used to soften the effect of requests or other statements in both spoken and written English. Read the following examples taken from MICASE and COCA and discuss the effect of hedgers (in bold).

Hedger	Corpus example	Your sentence
Parenthetical verbs (I think, I know, I suppose)	You wouldn't happen to have anything like a fig newton or a granola bar with you, **I suppose**? (COCA/FIC:SciFi)	
Modal or semi-modal verbs (could, would, might)	(On the phone) . . . **Could** you please check see whether you have uh, eight five? **Would you mind** checking because, what? I'm sorry, what is that? (MICASE/Service Encounters, Transcript ID: SVC999MX104)	
If-clauses (if you don't mind; if it is not too much trouble)	(request for explanation) . . . What, **if you don't mind** me asking like, what's the comparison of like, your wages? (MICASE/Student Presentation, Transcript ID: STP545JU091)	

(continued overleaf)

Hedger	Corpus example	Your sentence
Adverbs of likelihood (possibly, by any chance)	Do you know what time it is, **by any chance**? (COCA/SPOKEN: ABC Primetime Live)	
Adverbs of degree (a bit/a little, sort of/kind of)	. . . Can you think of a way of, just, um, how can I say this, of making that sentence **a little** more pointed? (MICASE/Office Hours, Transcript ID: OF-C300JU149	
Apology expressions + but (Sorry to bother you . . .)	Excuse me, **I'm sorry to bother you**. I have to make a really important call. Do you have a quarter to spare? (COCA/ SPOKEN:NBC Dateline)	

B ILLUSTRATE – In the table above, write your own sentence to illustrate the use of a hedger in each category. Share the sentences with your partner.

Activity 3: Now Let's Play!

A MAKE A REQUEST – On a slip of paper, write down a request statement starting with "I wish I/you could . . ." related to your classmates.

Example: **I wish I could** borrow your skateboard.

Then, fold the slip and put it in the box called the Box of Wishes.

B SOFTEN YOUR REQUEST – Pick up a slip from the Box of Wishes. Read the request statement and make a softened direct request to your classmate. Make sure you use the hedgers you reviewed in the previous activity:

Example: **Do you think** I **could** borrow your skateboard **for a bit**?

C RESPOND – Your classmate should respond appropriately to the request.

Example: Sure. Here you go.

Make sure you exchange slips and roles with him/her and at least three other classmates.

UNIT 4
FINAL UNIT TASK

A ROLE-PLAY – Record two of the following role-play request situations. Make sure you make a face-to-face request (as person A) in one, and respond to one (as person B) in the other.

When making a request, make sure you:

a. make a pre-request
b. soften your request (using a hedger)
c. are polite.

When responding to a request, make sure you:

a. respond to the pre-request positively
b. decline the request, and
   i. apologize
   ii. provide reasons for the decline
   iii. offer to make it up, if possible
c. are polite.

	Person A	Person B
1.	Ask your friend to give you a ride to the shopping mall on Friday.	Your wife is using the car that day.
2.	You want to have an appointment with your academic advisor this week.	She is fully booked this week.
3.	Ask at the University Housing Office to verify your last bill. You think you were overbilled.	They are closing now.
4.	You need to have a driver's license. Ask at the Office of International Students Affairs if you can apply for a Social Security number.	In this US state, as an international student you need to show employment authorization in order to apply for a Social Security number.
5.	You are going to fly to Canada over the weekend to visit your friend. Ask your classmate if you can borrow his carry-on bag.	He had left it at home the last time he visited his family.

B **EVALUATE –** Watch your recorded role plays. Use the following guidelines to evaluate your performance. How did you do?

Performance evaluation criteria	Yes	To some extent	No
Making a request:			
1. Did you use a pre-request appropriate to the situation and your relationship with the listener?			
2. Did you make a request appropriate to the situation and your relationship with the listener?		√	
3. Did you use polite language?			
Responding to a request:			
1. Did you decline the request appropriately (apologize, explain, and so on), according to the situation and your relationship with the listener?			
2. Did you use polite language?			
Overall performance:			
1. Did you speak fluently?			
2. Did you speak clearly?			
3. Was your language grammatically accurate?			
4. Was your performance natural?			

I would like to improve:

1. ______________________________

2. ______________________________

UNIT 4 SELF-ASSESSMENT: What Progress Did I Make?

1 Review Unit 4 vocabulary list and complete the table below.

	Expressions I can actively use	Expressions I need to review
Part 1: Make and respond to direct requests		
Part 2: Make and respond to indirect requests		
Part 3: Soften requests		

II These are the conversation strategies you practiced in this unit. Check (✓) the box in the category that best evaluates your ability to use them.

Strategy	Very well	Fairly well	Not very well
I can make a pre-request	☐	☐	☐
I can make a direct face-to-face request	☐	☐	☐
I can respond to a direct face-to-face request	☐	☐	☐
I can make a request on the phone	☐	☐	☐
I can make an indirect request	☐	☐	☐
I can respond to an indirect request	☐	☐	☐
I can soften a request by using hedgers	☐	☐	☐

III Write about what you learned in this unit, and what you plan to continue to work on:

One new skill/strategy I learned in this unit is:

____

____

What I plan to continue to work on is:

____

____

UNIT 4
VOCABULARY LIST

Use the chart below to study the new unit vocabulary and record any new topic-related vocabulary from this unit and elsewhere.

Topic/Function	Vocabulary to review	New vocabulary
Pre-request expressions	Can you do me a favor? Would you do me a favor, please? Hey, do me a favor . . . Do you have any plans this weekend? I was wondering if I could ask you a favor. Are you terribly busy this Saturday?	You got a minute? Sorry, can I bother you for a minute/ sec?
Request expressions	Can I/you . . . ? Could I . . . ? How about . . . ? Do/Would you have . . . ? Is it OK if I . . . ? Do you mind if I . . . ? Would you mind if I . . . ? Would you be willing to . . . ? I was wondering if I/you . . .	Paper or plastic? For here or to go? Do you by any chance have . . . ? Would you happen to . . . ? Do you think you could possibly . . . ?

Topic/Function	Vocabulary to review	New vocabulary
Expressions to accept a request	Absolutely. Definitely. Sure. Of course. OK. No problem/Not a problem. If you want to. I would be happy to. Glad to help. My pleasure.	Sure thing. For you? Sure.
Expressions to decline a request	Sorry, but I . . . I'm sorry I can't because . . . Well, I wish I could, but . . . You see, the thing is . . . Well, I hate to say "no," but . . . I would like to (help you), but I can't because . . . I'm afraid I can't because . . .	I can't believe I'm saying this, but I'm gonna (going to) have to say "no."
Request-softening expressions	I think/I know/I suppose Could/would/might . . . ? If you don't/wouldn't mind, . . . If you have (some) time, . . . Actually A bit/a little Sort of/kind of	If it is not/wouldn't be too much trouble . . . Could you possibly/by any chance . . . ? Would it be possible for you to . . . ? Sorry to bother you, but . . .

UNIT 4
QUIZ

Activity 1

Listen to the response to a direct request in these conversation extracts. Write down an appropriate direct request. Student A's direct request should match Student B's response.

Listening file: Unit_4_Quiz_1.mp3

1.	(Student A's parents arrive at the airport this weekend.) **A:** **B:** Actually, I need the car this weekend. I'm going to Chicago with my family. Sorry!	**3.**	(Student A is moving out.) **A:** **B:** I'd be happy to help. When do you need me to be at your house? Should I bring a friend, too?
2.	(Student A needs her friend's iPad) **A:** **B:** Sure, that's fine. I might need it this evening, though.	**4.**	(Student A missed the English class today) **A:** **B:** No problem. Just text in the evening to remind me, and I can send them to you by email.

Activity 2

Listen to the following requests. Choose the right response to match each of them.

Listening file: Unit_4_Quiz_2.mp3

1.	**A:** Do you happen to have change for a five? **B:** a. Sure, here you go. b. No, who are you? c. No, I don't happen. Sorry.	**3.**	**A:** For here or to go? **B:** a. I won't go. I need coffee. b. For here, please. c. For to go, please.
2.	**A:** I was wondering if I could borrow your bike for a half hour? **B:** a. Why do you need it? b. Where is your bike? c. Sorry, I need it to go to class.	**4.**	**A:** Do you mind if I use your manual for a sec? **B:** a. No, go ahead, please. b. Yes I do. Where is yours? c. It would be my great pleasure.

Activity 3

Listen to the following requests. Choose at least one hedger (softening word or phrase) from the table below to soften each request.

Listening file: Unit_4_Quiz_3.mp3

could/would/might	sort of/kind of
If you don't mind/If it is not too much trouble	Sorry to bother you but . . .
a bit/a little/quite/just	I think/ I know/I suppose

Request	Hedged (softened) request
1. (To roommate) Turn down this darn TV!	
2. (To classmate) You should help me with my homework.	
3. (To teacher) We expect you to give us our essay grades this week.	
4. (To teacher) Wait, please! I'll go and get it.	
5. (To classmate) Will you take care of my dog over the weekend?	
6. (To neighbor) Can you take care of my plants this month?	

Activity 4

Match each indirect request with an appropriate response. There is one extra response.

	Indirect request	Response
1.	(At a dorm room) I really can't seem to focus today. I didn't get much sleep last night. _____	**a.** Yes, but I will leave earlier today. Sorry.
2.	(In the classroom) Wows, it's a bit chilly, isn't it? _____	**b.** No, only weekends. Do you need it?
3.	(In the office) Did you drive today? _____	**c.** Really? Let me close the window then.
4.	(In a study group) I feel a bit tired now. _____	**d.** Sorry. I will turn the TV off in a minute.
5.	(Before class) Do you use your bike every day? _____	**e.** My pleasure!
		f. OK, let's have a break then.

LISTENING TRANSCRIPTS FOR *CAMPUS TALK*, UNITS 1–4

UNIT 1:
Connecting with each other

Unit 1, Part 1, Activity 1B: Let's Get Started

B **LISTEN AND IDENTIFY** – Susan is having a party at her place with some of her new school friends. Listen to their conversations. In pairs, identify and complete the table below with examples of conversation-opening words and phrases:

1. NIAMH, SALVADOR, CINDY, NICK

Niamh: Hi, I'm Niamh. How're you guys doing?
Salvador: Good. I'm Salvador. From Spain.
Niamh: Nice to meet you, Salvador.
Cindy: I'm Cindy. Hi.
Niamh: Hi, Cindy.
Nick: I'm Nick, from Canada. Where are you from, Niamh?
Niamh: Ireland.
Nick: Oh, wow! Are you in the same program with Susan?
Niamh: No, I'm at law school. What about you?
Nick: Me? Oh, (*laughs*) I'm here for the food.

2. LEE, BOB

Lee: Dude, what's up?
Bob: Not much. What's up with you? Haven't seen you in a long time.
Lee: I've been traveling. I didn't tell you, did I? I rented a car and drove it down the West Coast!
Bob: Seriously? How long did it take you?

3. GEORGE

George, Susan's husband (*on his cell phone*):
Hi Sam, this is George, Susan's husband. She asked me to call you to make sure you have a ride to the party. No? Well, I can come pick you up if you want. Yeah? In about ten minutes? Oh, okay, okay. In front of the computer lab? Okay, great, okay. See you in a bit!

4. LEON, SARA

Leon: Hi, there. This is Susan's place, right?
Sara: Yeah, come on in! You can drop your coat here if you want.
Leon: Sure. I'm Leon, by the way.
Sara: Sara.
Leon: Sara, you don't want to know . . . I got in the wrong apartment downstairs . . . So (*lengthens the vowel*) embarrassing!

5. NICKY, TRUDI

Nicky: Hey! We're in the same class, right?
Trudi: Yes, I think we are. Sorry, I don't know your name.
Nicky: Nicky. You're Trudi?
Trudi: Yes. Good memory! (*laughs*)
Nicky: My best friend in high school was called Trudi.
Trudi: Oh.

6. JO, ALICE

Alice: Jo, look at you! That's so awesome!
Jo: You like it?
Alice: I love it!

Unit 1, Part 1, Activity 4A: Forms of Address – What Else Can They Tell You?

A LISTEN AND INFER – Listen to each dialogue between various speakers in different situations. Analyze the language they use and check the appropriate box to describe each speaker's relationship to the listener. The first one is done for you.

1.

A: [*finds a big mess in his dorm room*] Guys! What's going on here?
B: Nothing, just trying to get rid of stuff!

2.

A: You guys! You really shouldn't have. Thank you so much!
B: No problem! Enjoy!

3.

A: I'm going to be honest with you, buddy. You really shouldn't have said anything.
B: Oh, come on! No big deal!

4.

A: Hey buddy, are you lost?
B: [*crying*] I can't find my Mommy!

5.

A: Dude, how much time do we have left?
B: Two minutes only! Hurry!

6.

A: Dude! Just chill, OK?
B: I really can't stand it when people cut in line like this!

7.

A: Hey man, watch out. Those things can walk, you know. [*the other person forgot her iPhone on the counter*]

B: Oops! Thanks!

8.

A: You can't do this to me, man! Why didn't you tell me?

B: Just didn't want to bother you.

9.

A: Excuse me, is this the way to the Lincoln Museum?

B: [*police officer*] Yes, Ma'am. Just keep right.

10.

A: Mom, I'm late! Is the sandwich ready?

B: Yes, Ma'am! Here you go!

Unit 1, Part 2, Activity 1A: Talking About What's New

A LISTEN AND RESPOND – Linda and Janet are drinking sodas and chatting at a campus café. Listen to the conversation and answer the following questions:

1. What is the relationship between the speakers?
2. What does Janet say to break the news to Linda?

Linda:	Guess what? My parents booked a ski vacation in Nevada.
Janet:	For real? That's fantastic! When are you going?
Linda:	We're going for a week at Christmas. It's just, like, my parents and me, and we're going to stay at Lake Tahoe.
Janet:	Awesome! Oh, I'm so jealous.
Linda:	And we'll be back in time for that New Year's Eve party that you and I are going to . . .
Janet:	Oh, um, I don't know how to tell you this, but . . .
Linda:	Hey, don't tell me you're not coming now . . .
Janet:	I'm really sorry but, um, I'm not going to be able to make it to that party. My grandma's having surgery on December 28th, and I want to be with her and, er, take care of her.
Linda:	Oh, I'm so sorry, Janet. I hope it's nothing serious.
Janet:	Thanks. No, nothing major. But I just want to be there for her.
Linda:	Yeah, I totally understand.

Unit 1, Part 2, Activity 3A: Ellipsis – Let's Make It Real

A **LISTEN AND DISCUSS –** Listen to this news-sharing conversation between friends. Does it sound natural? Why? Discuss this with you partner.

A:	Do you know I have good news to share with you?
B:	No, I don't know. What is the good news?
A:	The college gave me a research assistantship for the spring semester!
B:	This is really good news! I congratulate you on it.
A:	Thank you. I am also happy because I do not have to teach again next semester.
B:	Oh, yes, I understand how you feel about teaching. It is always an exhausting effort. That is great!
A:	Thank you. I have to go now. My class will start in a few minutes. I hope to see you later.
B:	Yes, I understand it. I will see you around.

Unit 1, Part 3, Activity 1A: Let's Review: Small Talk Topics

A **LISTEN AND INFER –** Ani is waiting for some friends at a coffee shop when she runs into Mathew, her classmate. They make small talk. Listen to their conversation and write down their small talk topics. What do you think motivates their choice of topics? Check (√) the right box/es below.

Mathew: Hey! How're you doing?
Ani: OK. You?
Mathew: Not too bad. Waiting for someone?
Ani: Yeah, I'm meeting up with some friends. You know, Jessica and Paul.
Mathew: Oh. What are you guys up to?
Ani: Nothing. We're going to hang out for a while, just chill.
Mathew: Right. Best place to be on a day like this. The weather's been just crazy!
Ani: Tell me about it! I am so ready for April! Anyway, what've you been up to?
Mathew: Nothing. Just studying. I had a bite and now, back to the library. I'm working on that paper for Professor Ryson.
Ani: The one on risk management?
Mathew: Yeah.
Ani: When exactly is it due? Do you know?
Mathew: Friday 5pm.
Ani: Oh, yeah! There's still plenty of time. So, what's your hurry? Got something planned for this weekend? What's her name? The one you're always hanging out with?
Mathew: [*laughs*] Emma? Nah! We're just buddies! Hey listen, got to run. I'll see you tonight at the gym, right?
Ani: Yep! I'll be there. Catch you later.
Mathew: OK. See ya!

1. Are the topics appropriate to the situation and participants? Explain why.
2. What other topics could be appropriate in this small talk? Name a few.
3. Do you consider Ani's question about Emma appropriate or inappropriate? Explain why.
4. Can you think of topics that would be inappropriate to bring up in such a conversation? Give examples.
5. How similar or different would topics in small talk between students be in your culture? Explain.

Unit 1, Part 3, Activity 2A: Keeping the Conversation Going – Focus on Strategies

A LISTEN AND IDENTIFY – Ani and her friends are hanging out at the Student Union after school. Listen to their conversation. Which of the following strategies do they use to keep the conversation going? Identify who uses the strategy (Ani, Jessica, Paul) in the first column in the table below. Include an example of what they do or say in the third column:

Paul: Hi there!
Ani: Oh, hi, guys.
Jessica: Wow, funky hat! [*picks up Ani's hat from the table*]
Ani: [*snatches her new hat back from Jessica and puts it on*] Isn't that cute? And it's so warm! So, you guys been cramming for that exam?
Paul: Sure thing. Jessica and I were, like, going over the online notes, just to review a bit.
Ani: Yeah? I'm planning to do that later, too.
Paul: Anybody care for a drink?
Ani: Thanks, I got some coffee already.
Jessica: I'm going to go get some tea.
Ani: OK, I'll be here. [*Paul and Jessica leave to get the drinks*]

[*Paul and Jessica return*]

Paul: So, been to the new movie yet?
Jessica: Which one?
Ani: Falling Star?
Paul: Yep! That's the one.
Ani: I read a bit about it online. It's one of those personal redemption stories. Charlize Theron plays this selfish Hollywood star, who's gotten really up there by pushing everyone else out of her way.
Paul: Uh-huh.
Ani: Like, she talks people into liking her, and helping her, and then she just drops them.
Paul: Sounds like one of those movies, um, you feel you've already seen . . .

Ani:	Well, I don't know, but it's Charlize Theron!
Jessica:	Yeah, she's awesome!
Ani:	So, anybody wants to come see it with me?
Paul:	When?
Ani:	This weekend.
Jessica:	I can do Saturday.
Paul:	I will have to pass, guys. I'm going to the game up in Wisconsin this weekend.
Ani:	I guess it's gonna be Jess and me, then.
Jessica:	Yep, I'm in.
Paul:	You go, guys. It sounds like a chick flick, anyway [*laughs*]
Jessica:	[*joking*] Your loss!
Ani:	[*getting ready to leave*] So, we're all set for Saturday, then?
Jessica:	Yep, yep. Oops, forgot to ask you. Did you decide about San Francisco?
Ani:	Yeah, it looks like I'm going to be there for a few weeks.
Paul:	Oh, wow! Nice.
Ani:	What about you, Jess?
Jessica:	Me? No plans yet. I'll probably keep working part-time through the entire summer. Not like somebody [*smiles and looks at Paul*].
Ani:	Where are you headed to, Paul?
Paul:	Europe, for a change. [*smiles*]
Ani:	Europe? Seriously? You're so lucky! Where're you going?
Paul:	Paris, Berlin, and Prague.
Ani:	Get out!!

Unit 1, Part 3, Activity 3B: Let's Review: Ending the Conversation

B LISTEN AND DISCUSS – Now listen to the ending of their conversation. Is it very different from your completed conversation ending above? Discuss in pairs.

Ani:	Excuse me. [*looks at her cell phone*] That's Rob telling me he's waiting for me outside. Sorry, guys. Gotta go now.
Paul:	OK, later!
Jessica:	Take care!
Ani:	Bye! [*goes*]
Jessica:	[*looks at her watch*] Wow, it's 8 already.
Paul:	Oh, yeah?
Jessica:	Yeah, and I still have to stop at the grocery store. Gotta grab some food!
Paul:	Yeah, me, too. See ya!
Jessica:	Bye!

UNIT 2: Putting your heads together

Unit 2, Part 1, Activity 1B: Let's Get Started

B **LISTEN AND COMPARE** – Students discuss their group survey presentation assignment on friendship and dating. Listen and take notes. How different or similar is it to student group communication in your country? Make a list of differences and/or similarities. Share with a partner.

Gina:	So, do we want to look at the questions first?
Ben:	Let me pull them up (*tries to open the file on his laptop*). I hate this pop-up thing! There we go!
Sue:	Hmm, so let's see . . . So, guys, do we want to go with the given questions or come up with our own?
Ben:	I'm fine with them.
Emma:	I was thinking we could probably change question 4 only. It's a bit like, too general.
Gina:	So, what do you guys think?
Ben:	(*at the same time*) Hmm . . .
Sue:	Maybe we could like list specific places, like 'at a café', 'at a party', something like that.
Ben:	Yeah, we could do that. (*starts typing*) Something like this?
Emma:	(*at the same time*) Yep! I like it!
Gina:	(*at the same time*) Much better! Now, are we all good with rest of the survey questions?
Emma:	(*at the same time*) Yup! I'm good!
Sue:	(*at the same time*) Huh-Uh!
Ben:	(*at the same time*) Sure.
Gina:	(*reads the survey presentation assignment aloud*) So, ". . . ask four university students . . ." So, does each of us talk to four students?

Sue:	Yeah, it looks like.
Ben:	(*at the same time*) What? Like four students, four questions each?
Emma:	(*responding to Ben*) I guess.
Ben:	Oh man, that's a lot! Sorry guys but honestly, I don't think I can handle that AND the presentation prep. I have two rewrites for next Monday . . .
Gina:	Wow! That's crazy.
Sue:	(*at the same time*) No worries. If you can get us the data, I can work on the PPT.
Emma:	Yeah, no biggie, we can finish it up.
Gina:	(*at the same time*) Yeah!
Ben:	Thanks, guys, when do you want them?
Sue:	Can you guys send them to me by this weekend?
Ben:	I'm going to try!
Gina:	(*at the same time*) Sure!
Emma:	(*at the same time*) Yep!
Sue:	OK, done deal! So, once I'm done with the PPT, I will send you the link. Do you still want to meet sometime next week then?
Gina:	Yeah, we might need to decide who presents what.
Emma:	Oh yeah, good point.
Ben:	(*at the same time*) Sure, just text us then.
Sue:	Awesome. Will do.

Unit 2, Part 1, Activity 4A: Managing Turns in Conversation

A LISTEN AND ANALYZE – Students are working on a class assignment in a group. Listen to their conversation and take notes. Then, answer the following questions about their group communication.

Lisa:	OK, let's get going! We have fifteen minutes to get this done.
Jim:	Wait. What does it say again?
Val:	If you had to give up your cell phone or your computer, which one would you choose to and why?
Greg:	What? How boring is that! I'm . . .
Lisa:	Come on! So, it says "Think about the advantages and disadvantages of each before you decide which one to give up." Do we want to split and work on this in pairs?
Val:	Good idea! Do you want to work with Greg? I can work with Jim. Is that OK?
Greg:	Oh boy!
Jim:	I'm OK with that, but do we have enough time for that?
Val:	Hmm, what do you think, Greg?
Greg:	Whatever! I will never give up my cell, anyway . . .
Lisa:	Yeah, totally. Me, neither. I can do so much with my phone already, and . . .
Jim:	Wait. Are we talking of desktops or laptops? 'Cause I can totally agree that you can get much more out of a phone than out of a desktop computer!
Val:	Hmm, it doesn't say, but I guess laptops are more popular now. And you can store and organize stuff real easy on a laptop. I play a lot more with my phone, but I get all my work done on my laptop, you know.
Greg:	Well, yeah, but nowadays you can do a whole lot with some fancy phones, too. And, anyway, who stores stuff on computers anymore? That's what the Cloud is for!
Val:	Yeah, I know. So, it looks like we might all go for giving up the computer then?
Greg:	I told you!

Lisa:	Sure.
Jim:	OK.
Val:	Well, I'm fine with that, too. Er, do we still want to list the advantages and disadvantages of the cell phone? We have about five minutes before we share this!

Unit 2, Part 2, Activity 1A: Expressing Certainty/Uncertainty

A **LISTEN AND GUESS –** Listen to these conversations between various speakers in different situations. Focus on the phrase of certainty or uncertainty in bold in each conversation. What is the speaker trying to say? Circle one of the given choices.

Conversations
1. Bob left the room and slammed the door behind him. His roommates were surprised: A: What's with him? B: **I think** he is kind of upset.
2. I ran my bike into a tree. A woman tried to help me get up. She was concerned: A: Are you sure you'll be alright? B: **I guess** so.
3. Jim did not show up at the weekly book club meeting. His friends were worried: A: Not sure what happened to Jim. He's never late. B: **I bet** he's sick.
4. James came out of the staff meeting very disappointed. We were surprised: A: What's going on? B: **I don't know**, but I am so ready to quit!
5 Jane had to study for the finals and take care of her family alone. Her friend tried to comfort her: A: You cannot imagine what I'm going through! B: **I know**, it's hard . . .

Unit 2, Part 3, Activity 1A: Making Suggestions – Focus on Appropriateness

A LISTEN AND ANALYZE – Listen to these short conversations. Focus on the inappropriate suggestions in bold in each of them. Why are they inappropriate? Discuss in your group.

DIALOGUE 1: TWO FRIENDS

A: I'm moving to a new apartment. You have to help me!
B: Sure.

DIALOGUE 2: A'S ROOMMATE DOESN'T LOOK LIKE HE WANTS TO GO TO THE MOVIES

A: It would be best if you join me at the movies.
B: I'm afraid I have a lot of work to do. Thanks, anyway.

DIALOGUE 3: AT A PARTY

Host: You must eat more. Here, try this!
Guest: Thanks! I am so full . . .

DIALOGUE 4: TWO CLASSMATES

A: I did not finish the assignment last night.
B: You should make more time.

DIALOGUE 5: BETWEEN FRIENDS

A: Wow, these cookies are so good, but I'm full.
B: Yeah, you had better stop eating cookies and go to the gym.

DIALOGUE 6: STUDENT AND TEACHER

A: OK, class, the quiz is over. Put your pencils down.
B: You've got to give us more time.

UNIT 3: Expressing yourself

Unit 3, Part 1, Activity 2A: Let's Review: Expressions of Joy and Enthusiasm

A LISTEN AND COMPLETE – Students are sharing exciting news. How do they respond to the news? Listen and complete each response turn with the expression of surprise, joy or enthusiasm that you hear.

CONVERSATION 1

A: Did I tell you? I got a summer internship in Chicago!
B: Wow, good for you!

CONVERSATION 2

A: I'll be travelling to Tokyo to attend a conference next month. My first time in Japan!
B: Fantastic! I'm happy for you.

CONVERSATION 3

A: I finally got a new laptop. Do you want to see it?
B: Oh wow! I love it!

CONVERSATION 4

A: Guess what! I got admission in the PhD program in business at this university!
B: Oh my God! How cool is that! Congratulations!

CONVERSATION 5

A: Did I tell you that I'm volunteering to build a new community center?
B: That's wonderful! How thoughtful of you.

CONVERSATION 6

A: I got a free ticket for the game.
B: Awesome! You lucky dog!

CONVERSATION 7

A: I didn't get a chance to tell you, but I finally got the new visa.
B: That's terrific! You must be so relieved.

Unit 3, Part 1, Activity 3B: Expressing Empathy

B LISTEN AND IDENTIFY – Jenny has just returned from a conference abroad. She and her friends are chatting at the gym.

Listen to the story Jenny shares with them. Number the expressions of empathy in the order you hear them. Not all the expressions will be used. The first empathy expression ("Oh, I'm so sorry!") is marked.

Amber:	Hey, Jenny, how are you? I haven't seen you in a while.
Jenny:	Oh, hi, Amber. Yeah, I need to catch up. I'm still a bit tired and slow.
Emily:	Oh, I'm so sorry. Have you been sick?
Jenny:	Sick? Oh, no, no. I guess I didn't get to tell you guys. I just came back from a conference in Europe. I'm still very jetlagged.
Amber:	Oh, no wonder! How was the conference?
Jenny:	The conference was great, but I had a crazy experience before the conference.
Emily:	Oh, no. What happened?
Jenny:	Well, I had to apply for a visa, believe it or not. Mail the passport, and all that.

Emily: That's a pain, isn't it?

Jenny: Oh yeah, more than you can imagine. I was supposed to fly last Sunday and I didn't have my passport with the visa yet on Saturday.

Amber: What? Are you kidding me? What a shame.

Emily: You must have been really stressed out.

Jenny: Oh, totally. I went to the post office, but they didn't have any mail for me.

Amber: That's horrible. What did you do?

Jenny: Well, they sent me to the Central Post Office out of town.

Emily: That's nuts! They get millions of packages every day there. I bet they thought you were joking.

Jenny: No, they were really sorry, but they told me that chances to find my passport overnight were very slim.

Emily: Oh, Jenny. I can imagine how you must have felt. Did you get to sleep that night?

Jenny: Not really. I was feeling miserable . . .

Amber: I would have been devastated. So, did you get to go a few days later then?

Jenny: No, you won't believe this, but at 4am that morning I got a call from the Central Post Office. They had found my passport!

Emily: Get out! They did? How cool is that!

Amber: Oh my God, Jenny. I still can't believe they did.

Jenny: Me, neither! I packed like crazy, and a friend gave me a ride to the airport! And that was it. I was there and had my presentation the first day of the conference.

Amber: Thank goodness for kind people!

Jenny: Oh yeah, I can't thank them enough.

Emily: Can you believe that? I am so happy for you, Jenny!

Unit 3, Part 1, Activity 4A: Expressing Sympathy and Sorrow

A **LISTEN AND IDENTIFY** – Listen to the expressions of sympathy and sorrow in the table below. While listening, check (✓) the ones you have heard or used before. Complete the table with an example of a situation each expression can be used in. Note: Some expressions can be used in multiple situations.

I have used/ heard this before	Expression of sympathy and sorrow	Situation
	I am so sorry about it.	
	I will be thinking of you.	
	I'm so sad to hear about . . .	
	I heard about . . . and I am extremely sorry.	
	My condolences.	
	I heard what happened. My deepest sympathy.	
	I can't believe that happened to you.	
✓	I hope you get better soon.	To wish someone sick a quick recovery
	I want you to know that I'm here for you.	
	Sorry you are going through this.	

Unit 3, Part 1, Activity 4C: Expressing Sympathy and Sorrow

C LISTEN AND MATCH – As we have seen in this unit, the expression "I'm sorry" (used to apologize) often indicates empathy, sympathy, regret, and other, depending on the context. A helpful way to identify its meaning is to identify the context and listen to the intonation this expression is spoken with. Listen to the following conversations made in various situations. Match the meaning of "Sorry/I'm sorry" with each situation. Share with your partner. One match is done for you.

	Situation
1. __	A: Excuse me. B. I'm sorry. (Moves away from the bus door)
2. __	A: I'm so sorry. I missed the bus. B. You're good. It's just 5:01.
3. __	A: You need to pay the library fine before you can borrow another book. B: I'm sorry?
4. __	A: My cat died over the weekend. B: I'm really sorry. I know how much you loved her.
5. __	A: Sorry, is this seat taken? B: No, I don't think so.
6. __	A: I have a terrible headache. B: I'm sorry.
7. _e_	A: That's a terrible thing to say. B: I'm sorry you feel that way.
8. __	A: I'm sorry? B: At 8am, not 9am.

Unit 3, Part 2, Activity 2B: Expressing Anger

B **LISTEN AND DISCUSS** – At a school dorm, two students are talking about their roommate. Listen and answer the following questions. Discuss your answers with your partner.

Chris:	Hey roomie, how did it go?
Karen:	It's done.
Chris:	Was it as difficult as you expected?
Karen:	Yeah, sort of, but it's over. I don't want to talk about it.
Chris:	You must be tired.
Karen:	Yeah, I am sick and tired of trying to keep this room in a good shape.
Chris:	What's wrong? What happened?
Karen:	When I came back from school, the room was totally trashed. Becky's stuff was all over the floor and on my bed. The bathroom was flooded. It was a disaster!
Chris:	Hmm, why does she keep doing that? Was she running late for school?
Karen:	I couldn't care less. She doesn't live alone. I really can't take it anymore. I will talk to the RA and move out.
Chris:	Have you talked to Becky about it?
Karen:	More than once. It's just a waste of time. She says "I'm sorry" and then does it again. I can't stand it any longer.
Chris:	Yeah. That's disappointing. Let me talk to her. I'm sure we can handle this. Hey, by the way, do you want to join us? We want to go get the posters this afternoon.
Karen:	Thanks. You guys go ahead. I'm going to try and sleep this off.

UNIT 4: Getting things done

Unit 4, Part 1, Activity 1A: Let's Get Started

A **LISTEN AND DISCUSS –** Listen to the students' requests in the conversations below. Every request is inappropriate. Discuss each conversation with your partner and consider the situation and the speaker–listener relationship.

1. At the end of class

A student has questions about his quiz errors:

Teacher: Would you like to make an appointment to go over the quiz together, then?

Student: Yes. Thank you. Let me visit your office on Wednesday.

2. At the international student advisor's office:

A student finds the door open and walks into the international student advisor's office:

Student: Hi, my friend told me that I should see you. I will go to Canada. Can you sign my I-20 now?

Advisor: Well, . . .

3. At the end of the quiz

A student is asking when the quiz will be graded:

Teacher: OK, time is up. Please turn in the quizzes, everybody.

Student: (*handing in the quiz to the teacher*) How about the grades?

4. At the academic advisor's office

A student is inquiring about sources of funding to support her studies:

Academic advisor: Have you thought about applying for a research assistantship?

Student: I am not sure. Can you give me an assistantship for next semester?

Unit 4, Part 1, Activity 4A: Making Face-to-face Requests

A **LISTEN AND ANALYZE –** Listen to the response to each of the following request situations. Based on the response, are the situations formal or informal? Circle F for formal and I for informal. The first one is done for you.

1. **You want to borrow your friend's electronic dictionary.** F (I)

   A: Can I borrow your dictionary?

   B: Sure. Here you go.

2. **You need a two-day extension to complete your paper in the Psychology class.** F I

   A: I'd like to ask for a two-day extension for this paper.

   B: I normally do not give extensions. Is there a problem?

3. **You need to return a sweater in the store.** F I

   A: I want to return this sweater.

   B: Was anything wrong with it?

4. **You want to borrow your neighbor's car Saturday evening.** F I

   A: I've got a favor to ask – my car is in for repairs, and so I was wondering if I could borrow your car this weekend.

   B: Well, I hate to say "no", but I'm going to need it on the weekend. I'm going out of town. Sorry!

5. **You need to register for the aerobics class but the registration deadline was the day before.** F I

   A: I would like to register for the beginners' aerobics class.

   B: Sorry but the registration deadline has passed, and the class is full.

6. **You need to call the doctor, but you discover you left your phone at home. Ask your classmate to lend you his.** F I

   A: Hey, can I use your phone? I gotta call my doctor and I've left my phone at home.

   B: OK. I hope they don't put you on hold for life . . . Just kidding!

7. **You want to get coffee at the university library's café**. F I

   A: A macchiato.

   B: For here or to go?

8. **You need a ride to the city airport at noon tomorrow. Ask your new friend to help you with it.** F I

   A: Say, would you be able to give me a ride to the city airport at noon tomorrow?

   B: Tomorrow? I'm sorry, I'm afraid I can't make it. I just made lunch plans with a friend.

Unit 4, Part 1, Activity 5B: Making Requests on the Phone

B LISTEN AND MAKE A REQUEST – You need to request information or a service by phone. Listen to the telephone prompt. Write down a greeting or introduction followed by an appropriate request. Here is an example:

What you hear: Hampton Inn. How can I help you?

What you may say: This is room 305. Can you give me a wake-up call tomorrow at 6am, please?

1. McHenry Health Center. How can I help you?
2. Alpha Systems. How can I help you?
3. One West Apartments. How can I help you today?
4. Cotton World. How can I help you?
5. Carle Apartment Maintenance. How can I help you?
6. University Student Services. How can I help you?
7. "One for You" flower shop. How can I help you?
8. University library. How can I help you?

Unit 4, Part 2, Activity 1A: Identifying Indirect Requests

A **LISTEN AND ANALYZE –** Students are ordering lunch on a hot summer day. Listen to their conversations. How are requests being made? How do students respond to each of them? Underline all requests and responses. Discuss them with your partner.

Ben:	Oh man, it's so crowded here!
Lisa:	Yeah. And it's really noisy! I want to try a different place.
Peter:	Sure. I love the little Indian place next to the dorm.
Jen:	Yeah, that's a cute one. But I really want to check Gianni's. We still have time, right?
Lisa:	Yep, you're right! (*at the same time*)
Ben:	Oh, Gianni's, great choice! (*at the same time*)
Peter:	I wouldn't miss their pizzas, either. Let's go!

(*at Gianni's; students get a table under a big fan*)

Jen:	Oh my goodness, I'm going to be swept away before I know it!
Ben:	No kidding! There should be a way to turn it down a bit. (*to the approaching waiter*) Hi. Do you think it's possible to slow this down a tiny bit? It's kind of windy down here!
Waiter:	(*smiling*) Sure, no problem. Can I get you started with anything?
Lisa:	Yes, please. I'm really hot.
Waiter:	Water, lemonade, ice tea?
Lisa:	Just water with ice and lemon, please.
Jen:	Same here.
Waiter:	Sure.
Peter:	I'm dying for a freshly squeezed fruit juice.
Waiter:	Sorry, we only have bottled juices.
Peter:	Never mind then. Just get me a cold ginger ale.
Waiter:	For you?
Ben:	Iced tea with lemon, please.
Waiter:	OK, I'll be right back.

(*Students discuss the pizza menu choices*)

Lisa: I'm not too hungry. Do you want to split a pizza, Jen?
Jen: Absolutely! What's your favorite?
Lisa: Anything that doesn't have capers on it!
Jen: Sure! I've been curious about the fig and roasted walnut one.
Lisa: Yeah, that looks interesting. Let's try it! (*pointing to a big-sized pizza on a tray*) Oh, boy, look at that big one!
Jen: Yeah, that's humongous! Let's get a medium, shall we?
Lisa: Yeah, a medium should be fine.
Peter: Do you know what you're getting, Ben?
Ben: Hmm. Not sure yet.
Peter: I'll have a Pizza Margherita. Big!
Ben: Nice choice. That's what this place is famous for. I get it all the time.

(*Waiter brings the drinks*)

Waiter: Here you go. Are you guys ready to order?
Jen: We'll split a medium fig and roasted walnuts.
Peter: A big Margherita for me, please.
Waiter: OK, and for you?
Ben: Sorry, I'm a bit slow today.
Waiter: No problem. I'll give you a few more minutes.
Ben: No, no, no, thanks. Hmm, I'll have a spinach and artichoke, medium, please. Thanks!
Waiter: Great! That's very popular here. I'll be right back with your order.

Unit 4, Part 2, Activity 2A: Understanding and Responding to Indirect Requests

A LISTEN AND DISCUSS – The following conversations begin at a dorm. The speaker is trying to formulate an indirect request in each situation. Listen and discuss each speaker's indirect request statement with your partner.

Scene	Speaker's statement	Meaning
1. Dorm room (when noticing the roommate had not cleaned the room)	**Oh my God! This room is a total mess.**	
2. Cafeteria (when noticing someone cutting in line)	**What! He must be kidding me! (to the person cutting in line): Sorry, the line starts here.**	
3. Study room (when entering a non-air-conditioned room	**Is it me, or is it this room? I'm kind of hot.**	
4. Friend's party (when looking at cookies)	**Wow! These cookies look really yummy.**	
5. In front of the TV (when bothered by the loud volume of the TV)	**Boy, he is loud, isn't he?**	

Unit 4, Part 3, Activity 1: Understanding the Use of "Please"

DID YOU KNOW THAT . . . ?

We often believe that adding "please" makes a request sound more polite in spoken interaction. Take a look at the following:

1. **Correct my draft, please.**
2. **Send me the homework, please.**
3. **Show me my errors, please.**
4. **Check my statement of purpose, please.**
5. **Show me my attendance, please.**

Why aren't these statements polite? What can they tell you about the listener–speaker relationship they imply?

In fact:

- "Please" is more common in formal writing than in formal speech.
- When "please" occurs in formal speech, it is more often used with requests made on the phone in standard, routinized situations such as:
    1. asking the other person to wait in the line
    2. asking to speak to a special person
    3. asking somebody to call back
    4. leaving a message
    5. asking for an extension, a special department, a telephone number.
- "Could you" has been replacing "please" to show politeness in informal speech.

(Aijmer, K. *Conversational Routines in English: Convention and Creativity*. London and New York: Routledge, 2014)

A ANALYZE AND IDENTIFY – Listen to the request statement in each situation. Who is talking to whom? What is the speaker trying to say or do? Write down the possible meaning of "please" in each statement.

Example:

Request statement	**Meaning of "please"**
Please leave!	Warning.

Request statement	**Meaning of "please"**
1. Oh, please, Jack! For heaven's sake!	______________
2. Diet Coke, please.	______________
3. Next slide, please.	______________
4. Girls, please! Quiet!	______________
5. Yes, please?	______________
6. Would you please . . . (pauses in anger)!	______________

B LISTEN AND DESCRIBE – "Please" in requests can have various intonation patterns, depending on politeness, expectations, the speaker's intent and emotional state. In general, "please" in polite requests has a rising intonation. In an elevated emotional state, "please" can be realized with a falling intonation.

Now, go back to the request statements above. Listen and determine its intonation pattern in each statement:

1. Oh, please, Jack! For heavens' sake!	[Rising]	[Falling]
2. Diet Coke, please.	[Rising]	[Falling]
3. Next slide, please.	[Rising]	[Falling]
4. Girls, please! Quiet!	[Rising]	[Falling]
5. Yes, please?	[Rising]	[Falling]
6. Would you please . . . (pauses in anger)!	[Rising]	[Falling]

C LISTEN AND REPEAT – Listen again to each statement and repeat after the speaker.